DESIGNING A LAYOUT

BUILDING A MODEL RAILWAY

DESIGNING A LAYOUT

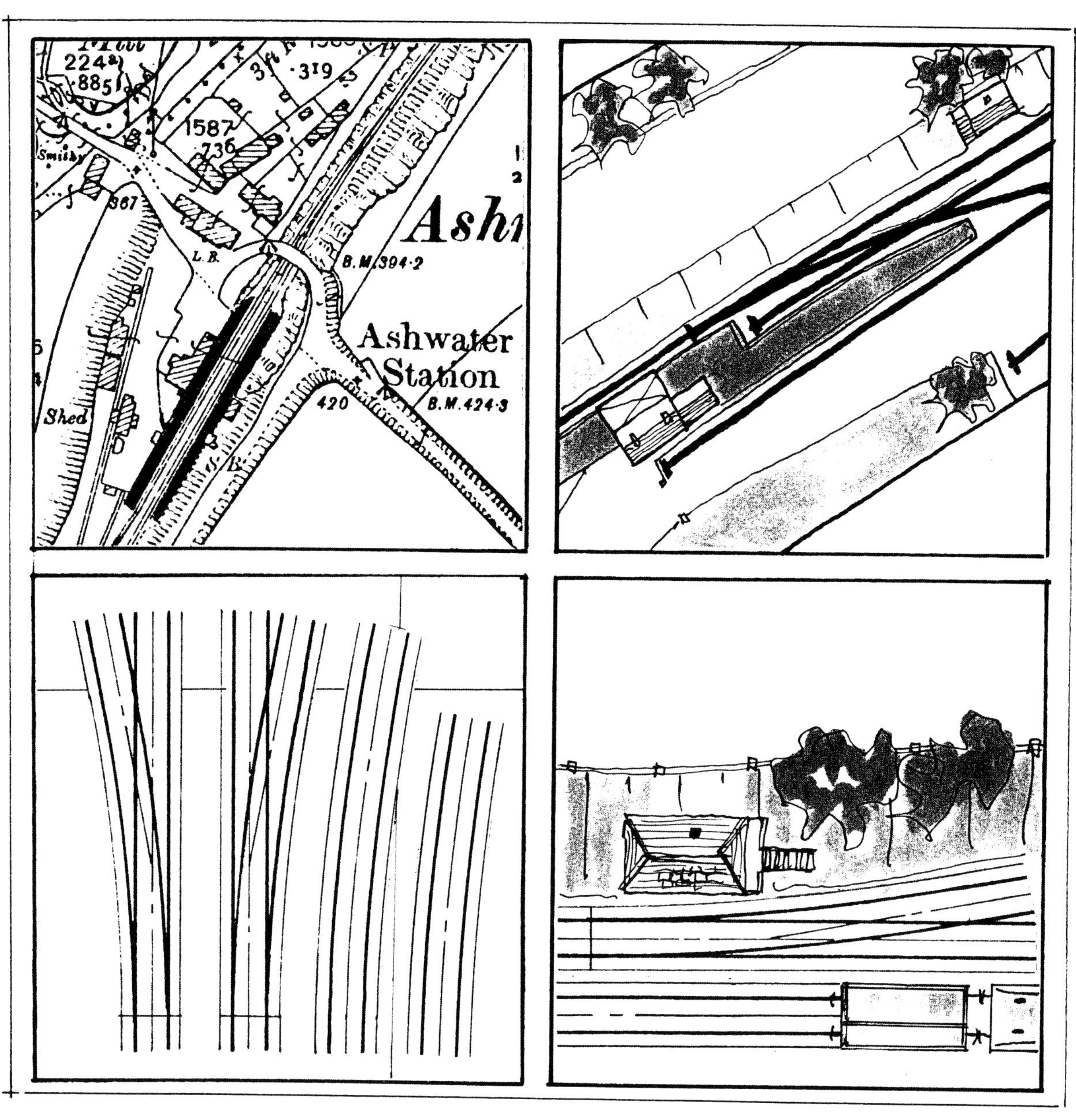

Barry Norman

ISBN 1 874103 39 9

Designed by Paul Karau
Printed by Amadeus Press Ltd., Huddersfield

Published by
WILD SWAN PUBLICATIONS LTD.
1-3 Hagbourne Road, Didcot, Oxon, OX11 8DP

FOR MY MUM AND DAD

CONTENTS

PART ONE
Designing a Layout

To me an interesting layout will paint a picture, not only of the locomotives and rolling stock of a past age but also of the wider scene in which they ran. When I modelled Lydham Heath, I was attracted by the atmosphere of the station and I wanted to say something about the neglect and sadness of this frail railway struggling to exist in a beautiful part of Shropshire. The rusting rails lying beneath weeds and withering grass were a poignant indication of the economic depression of the Bishops Castle Railway that was run only with

dilapidated second-hand rolling stock. It was this image of decline that provided the focus for all my thinking. I wasn't just trying to model the station as it may have been; I wanted more than that. I also wanted to encapsulate the atmosphere of the place. It is the atmosphere of a successful model which sets it apart from other layouts. Therefore, it is vital before you begin, to pin-point what you are trying to achieve. The quaintness of a light railway and the grandeur of the main line are quite different, and it is the realisation of what makes these differences which is the key to successful modelling of atmosphere. It is not sufficient, in my view, just to choose a station to model. It is important to interpret it so that you play upon the ideas and feelings the station conveys to you. The air of neglect attempted in my model of Lydham Heath is quite different from the atmosphere portrayed on my earlier model, 'Petherick'.

Here, nestling amongst rolling hills and refreshed by cool sea breezes lay a small station. One of little significance, it was lost in a landscape that was typically Cornish; one where I could imagine lying back in the sun, listening to the skylarks and endless crashing of distant waves beating against a rocky coastline. In the conception of 'Petherick', the mental picture which drove me was one of holiday excitement, the Atlantic Coast Express taking holidaymakers away from their humdrum lives for a fortnight. My boyhood memories of escaping annually from the noise and bustle of London, to drag sticks in the wet sand and skim smooth flat pebbles into the sea, were vivid in my mind.

The sunny days and fresh sea breezes of North Cornwall are sharply contrasted

I like to imagine the sound of clanking buffers ringing through the blackened alleyways of Inkerman Street, adding to the everyday scenes of life during the threatening years of World War II. This was the picture we had in our minds when building this 7mm scale model of what might have been seen in Salford.

at 'Inkerman Street', where the gloom of a northern city in the war years inspired the MRJ team. We wanted to hear the clanking of buffers echoing between the backs of terraced houses, and feel the dustladen wind gusting through smoke-blackened alleyways. It was to be an everyday scene: the corner shop, the local pub, and a busy urban station with its cobbled forecourt and cramped platform sheltered beneath a dingy canopy. Here, in contrast to seaside sunshine, was to be grimy urban gloom.

MODELLING A PARTICULAR PROTOTYPE

The starting point for any layout must be an examination of the prototype. However, for several reasons, it is not usually possible to model a prototype to true scale. Make no mistake, a station covers a large site, and if sufficient surrounding land is to be included to set the scene, the resulting model is often enormous. There is not usually enough room at home to build a model of a station in its entirety. In this case, platforms may need to be shortened and/or other parts left out. Once the initial deviation has been made (out of necessity), your conscience may allow you to take bigger liberties. Some of the ways in which I have done this are shown in the many examples in Part 2 of this book. I will make reference to these as I thread my way through the many ways in which a station can be altered, making it not only smaller, but also more challenging visually and interesting to operate.

Midhurst (page 69) is a good example of this. As a branch line terminus, this station was quite small, yet would scale about 17ft long in 4mm scale. This is unlikely to fit into the railway room, so it becomes necessary to modify the prototype plan, and in this instance it is easy to do. A reduction in the length of the sidings and run-round would pull closer together the main features of the station, the engine shed, goods shed, station building and platform, and the unusual signal box. The model would probably look better like this whilst retaining much of the character of the prototype and at the same time proving a much more manageable layout.

Working in 2mm scale (N gauge) is an obvious way of coping with a larger prototype station. The design on page 70 is based very closely on Chinley, and packs the excitement of a four-track main line into a mere 12ft. I believe it is a mistake to make too small a layout in this scale; the possibilities of modelling a main line in rolling moorland are just too tempting to resist. I am especially reminded of 'Chiltern Green', a masterful mix of landscape and railway, where the four tracks of London main line gave an exhibition-goer plenty to look at.

Having chosen a prototype, we are presented with the problem of finding enough suitable information to enable the model to be built. A site visit to a station, which may have been closed for some thirty years, will quite likely reveal little trace of the railway as it was, especially if it has been redeveloped as an industrial

Fig. 1

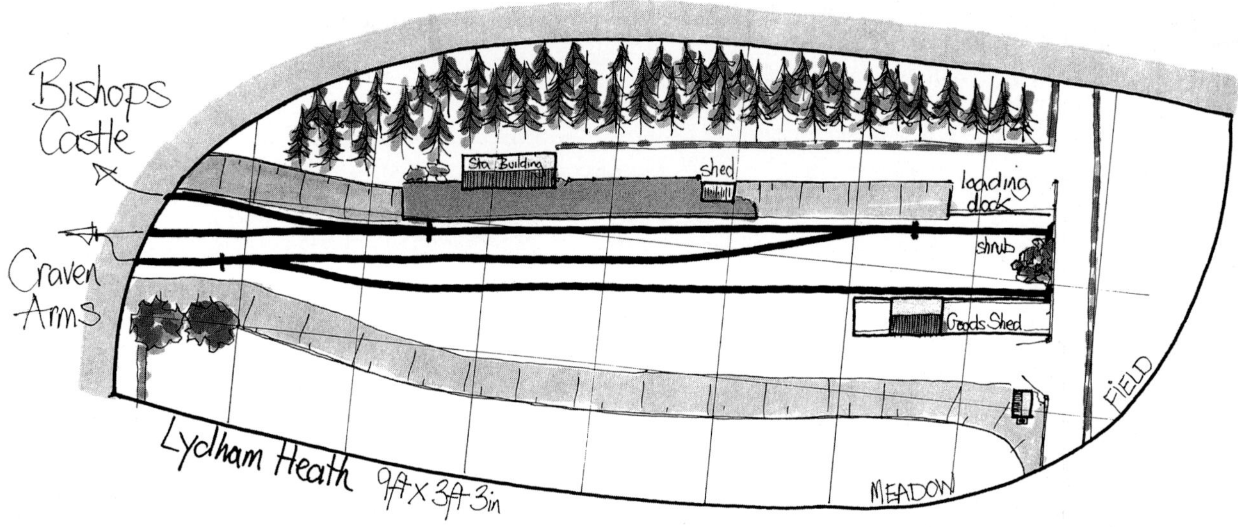

estate or suchlike. However, photographs do exist, although few places have been recorded thoroughly (why should anyone have wished to record every detail of a station all those years ago?). When I collected photographs of Lydham (*Fig. 1*) I still found that I had to make an educated guess at what some of the buildings looked like. There was good photographic coverage of the station building and, although little seems to have been known about the back wall, there was enough to make a reasonably accurate model (*Fig. 2*). However, without any actual dimensions available, I had to estimate the height of the guttering, the depth of the windows and the width of the ends. Proportion and logic play a key role in this kind of modelling, for, with a building demolished some fifty years ago, there is no alternative.

The weighbridge hut puzzled me for some time. I could not determine what it was built from. Was it timber or corrugated iron, and what was the roof made of? It only appeared in distant photographs, so I examined the other stations on the line and found a similar building at Horderley. This became the prototype for the model (*Fig. 3*).

The goods shed proved little easier. I only had a distant view of one end, and a shot of part of one side. The resulting model is very characterful, but perhaps this is because of the conjecture I had to employ (*Fig. 4*). Using such guesswork, the line between fact and fiction can become a little blurred. It therefore cannot be

Fig. 2

Modelling a particular prototype can be chastening as it relies on searching out period photographs, maps and, if you are lucky, drawings. I chose S scale in which to model this unusual station.

considered an accurate model of the station, although, in essence, I hope it captures some of the character and atmosphere of the place.

Some stations, whilst being interesting in parts, would, I feel, look very dull as a model. I think it is better to focus on the interesting areas, which has the added advantage of making the size of the model more manageable. With this in mind, I decided to reduce the length of Lydham by leaving out the loop entry turnout. I could see little operational value in keeping it (if I used the fiddle yard to shunt with), and scenically it would have needed even more pine trees to be made – there were more than enough of them already! Laziness apart, I feel the model looks better for shortening and loses nothing in character or operation.

In building this layout, I have learned to doubt the wisdom of modelling a prototype exactly. I wonder whether I

Despite the difficulty in finding enough information, I feel that this view quite closely reflects the appearance of the station.

Little photographic evidence was discovered to enable an accurate model of the goods shed. The resulting model is characterful, but was it like this?

Fig. 3

Fig. 4

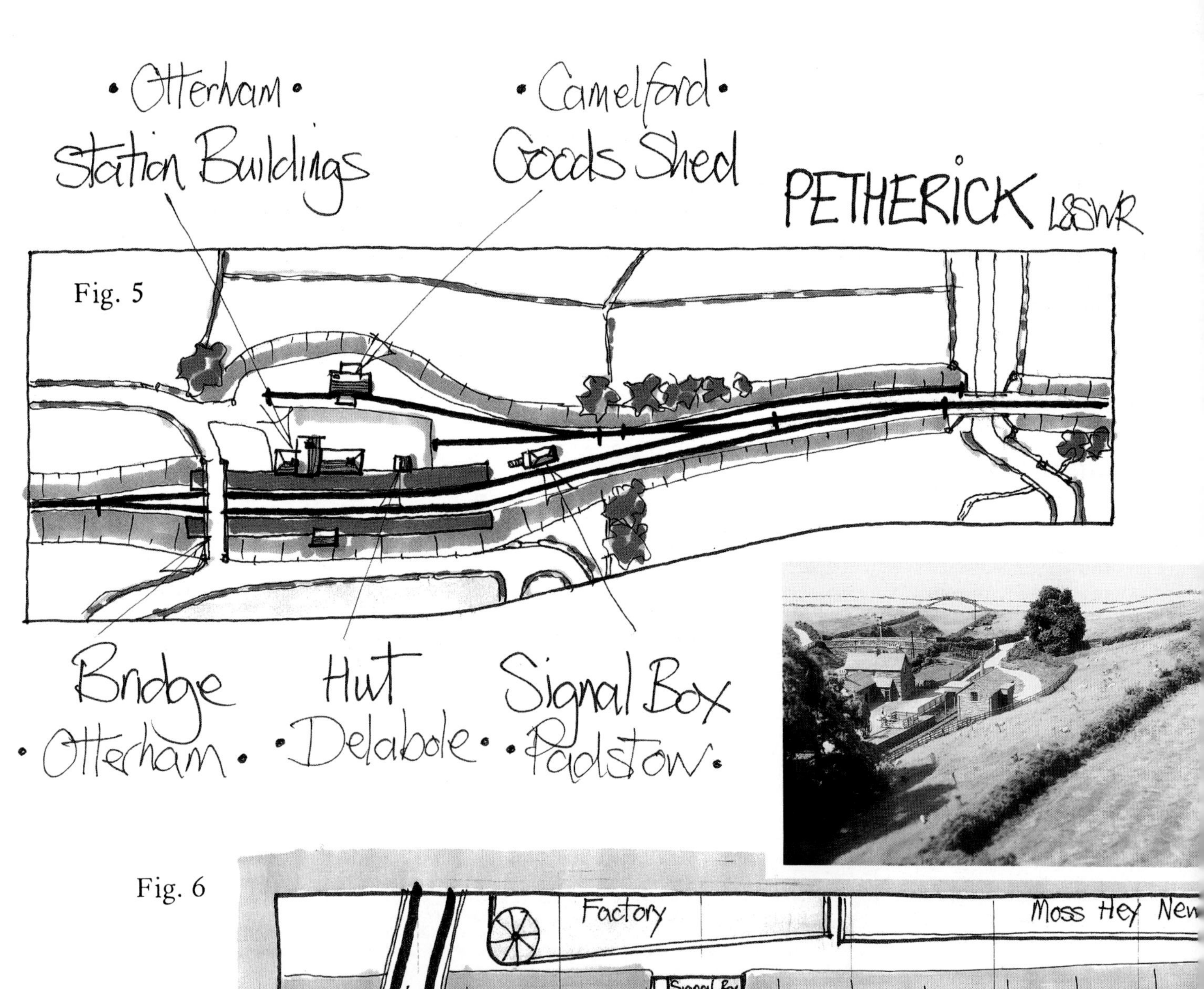

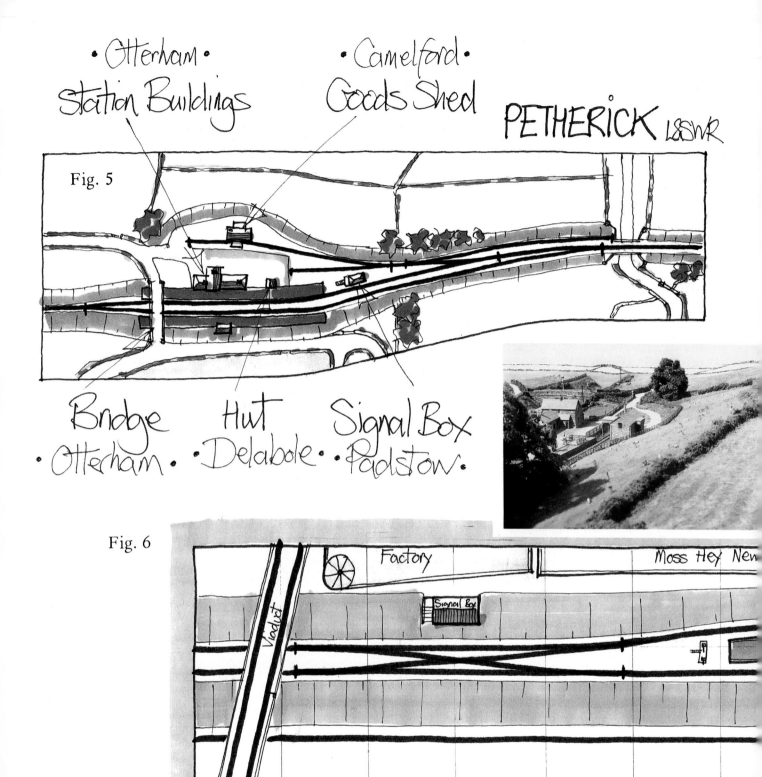

• Otterham •
Station Buildings
• Camelford •
Goods Shed
PETHERICK L&SWR
Bridge
• Otterham •
Hut
• Delabole •
Signal Box
• Padstow •

Fig. 5

Fig. 6

Factory
Moss Hey New
Signal Box
Viaduct
LNWR line
Inkerman Street Goods Y
7MM Scale
EACH SQUARE EQUALS
12" – 7mm scale
7" – 4mm scale

have built a model of Lydham Heath, or a model *based* upon Lydham Heath, but, either way, I do feel satisfied that I have captured the dilapidated atmosphere.

MIXING DIFFERENT PROTOTYPES

One station is rarely ideal. It may be too simple or too complex, have few buildings or too many, it may even lack a feature that you particularly would like to model (such as an engine shed). To cope with this dilemma, a practical solution is to mix two or more stations together. This was very much the approach I adopted when planning Petherick. I took the track plan from Otterham but put it in a setting modelled on the landscape around Whitstone and Bridgerule stations on the Bude branch. This crossbreed plan was not just a mixture of two stations, but also included all the things that I felt should be found at a station set in this part of Cornwall. Thus I was able to model a convincing stop on the LSWR North Cornwall line by including many of those things that I felt characterized that line, pinching bits from different stations (*Fig. 5*) and feeling free to exploit the full scenic potential of the Cornish geography.

This is not usually difficult to do, as on many branch lines a specific style of architecture is repeated at most, if not all, of the stations. It is therefore easy to pick parts from different stations, mix them together and produce a new station that fits harmoniously into the scheme of the rest. The Worth Valley Railway is another good example of this interchangeability, and it is this line, skirting the moors of Yorkshire, which is the subject of my design on page 72.

AN IMAGINARY PROTOTYPE

'Inkerman Street' (*Fig. 6*) falls into a third and last category, one where imagination reigns over prototype correctness. This can be fun, but it is best to keep a close eye on a prototype so that something too fanciful and unconvincing is not created. The track plan of 'Inkerman Street', although sketched out on the back of an envelope, was carefully conceived with a considerable understanding of how a railway would have been built. We researched several Lancashire & Yorkshire Railway stations and used photographs to piece together a suitable design for 'Inkerman Street'. The station was surrounded by everyday life where ordinary people were going about their ordinary jobs to the sounds of shunting in an urban goods yard. This and a Jinty trundling over the black and dusty track, with lines of coal wagons, were visions of the mundane, unspectacular scene we wanted to capture.

We decided which shops to model, which pub, which mill – there was plenty for one's imagination to do in composing the scene. I remember it took some time to agree on the type of structure that was to bridge the end of the layout. We knew it should be a railway viaduct of sorts, but thought that research and imagination were needed to make it happen. Likewise, Mr. Levine's yard was at one time to be an oil depot, but it ended up as a builder's yard, and we were pleased. However,

therick was a mixture of veral stations on the orth Cornwall line.

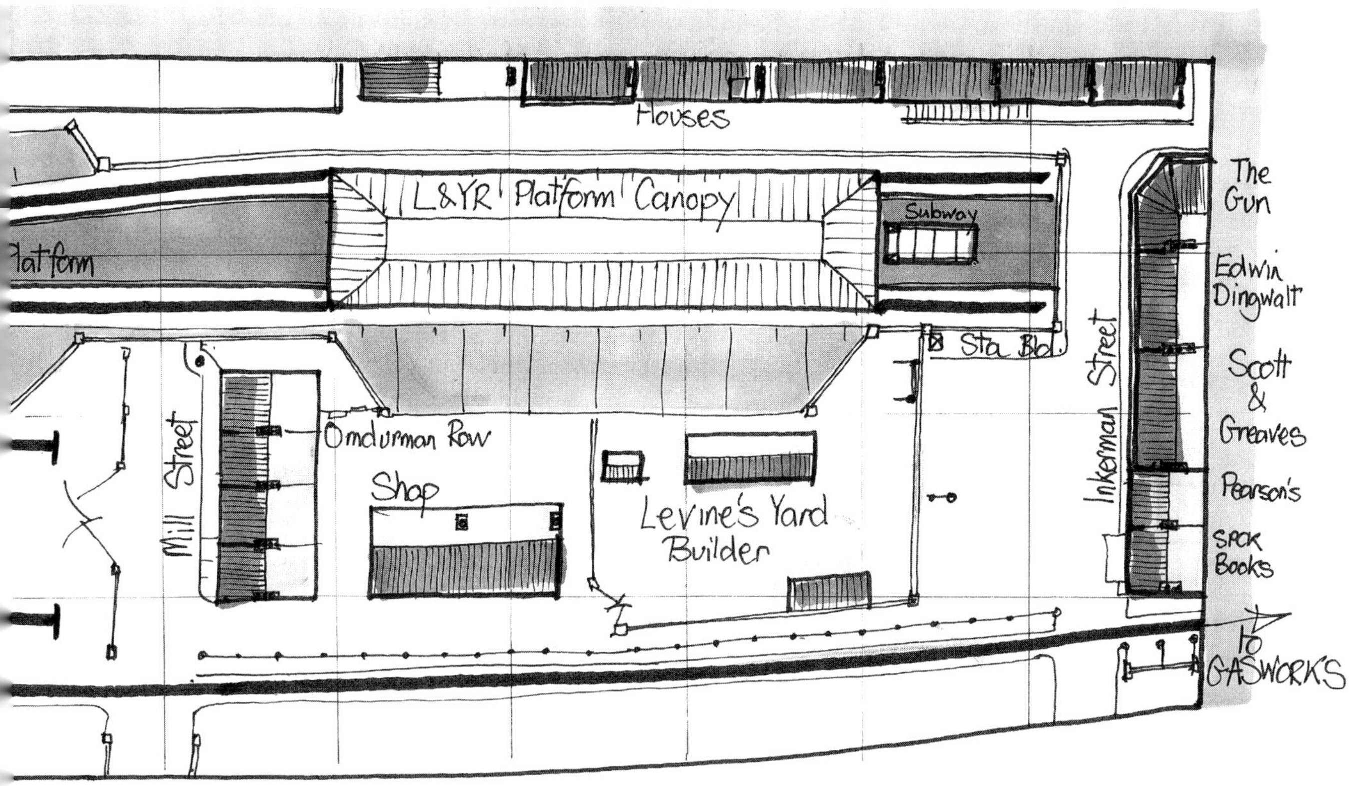

an imaginary design is not an easy option. It requires knowledge, ideas, research, inspiration and, above all else, a constant vision of what a railway company may have built. This type of layout is difficult to design well, and imaginary ones are frequently poorly produced, due, I feel, to a lack of a prototype discipline. This is not the case, though, in the next example which has a long history.

The county of Lyonesse was first mentioned in 1928 by A. G. Vercoe in *Model Railway News*, and the theme was later developed by Mr. Boyd Carpenter (1945) and finally by R. D. N. Salisbury who, in December 1964, showed his layout of that name in *Railway Modeller*. It was an imaginary kingdom which, as envisaged by Mr. Salisbury, was unspoilt by heavy industries or mining and relied solely upon tourism and farming for its wealth. I feel sure that if this delightfully wooded county really existed, it would never have a motorway or a drug problem!

One of my favourite examples of a layout crafted out of the imagination of its builder, is Bramblewick. Tom Harland's P4 model of a station in Robin Hood's Bay was inspired by a novel by Leo Walmsley, who wrote about the village using the pseudonym Bramblewick. Tom turned the idea into an NER station where one could watch the passing and shunting of trains during the summer of 1907.

The Lyonesse Railways were a perfect railway system to model, one that Mr. Salisbury went on to say ran through a 'rather conservative county, where there are no so-called modern attractions such as television, holiday camps, multiple shops or bingo halls'.

I often think that railway modelling is very much about escaping from our everyday lives into a world we might dream about. Certainly Lyonesse, of Arthurian legend, is a perfect release. Following this theme, I have devised my own Camelot and Tresco, basing them partly on real Cornish stations (page 74).

CHOOSING THE PROTOTYPE

I look for prototypes that have interesting features or unusual buildings (*Fig.* 7) that I feel I could exploit. Bishops Castle is one such example of this. The most unusual combination of engine and carriage sheds attracts the eye, especially in their very run-down and dilapidated state. It is an intriguing scene, that

Fig. 7

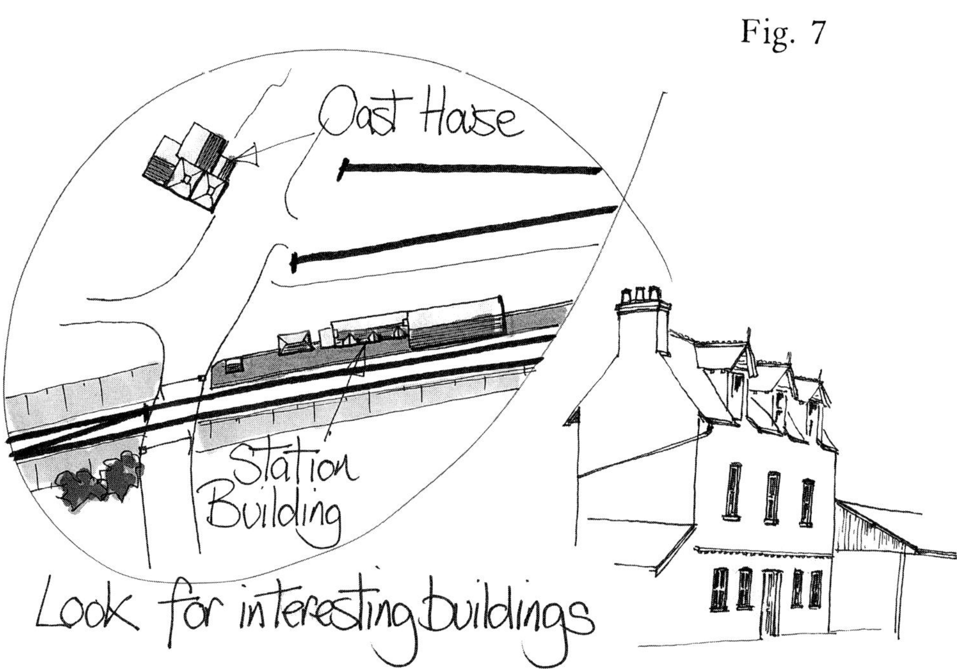

The county of Lyonesse and its imaginary railway inspired me to dream up my own interpretation of the myth. St. Ives became my Camelot and and the train in the picture would be waiting to depart for Tresco.

characterizes the essence of a light railway slowly withering towards closure (page 76). Similarly the train shed at Alnwick (page 77) first took my eye and became the dominant feature of the whole design.

It is frequently rewarding to look over the railway fence to see what other interesting features exist. The railway attracts industries, and these can offer us a powerful image of day-to-day life in the surrounding community. The Pennine textile mills huddled in the bleak borders of Yorkshire and Lancashire were connected to many lines. At Delph station, Bailey Mill stands behind the platform (*Fig. 8*). It reflects so well the location of the station and would, through its stone walls and mill chimney, focus the mind on the station's moorland neighbourhood. Similarly, the fading red of the brick-built Maltings at Hadleigh make us aware of the day-to-day business of the Suffolk station.

Both these stations benefited from their respective industries, which brought much trade. The inclusion of factories, gasworks, brickworks, potteries, quarries, wood-yards and quays in a model all add to the operational potential of the layout, as well as visual interest.

A stone yard could be found at the approach to Swanage station where local

The operation of a layout is greatly enriched by the addition of an industrial siding. Here the shunting of empty wagons into Leighswood brickworks or full milk tankers out of the dairy, would bring interest and new opportunities to a sequence of operation.
F. W. SHUTTLEWORTH

P. J. GARLAND

The maltings at Hadleigh provide not only a useful source of goods traffic, but also a very fine backdrop to this GER station. D. THOMPSON

Fig. 8

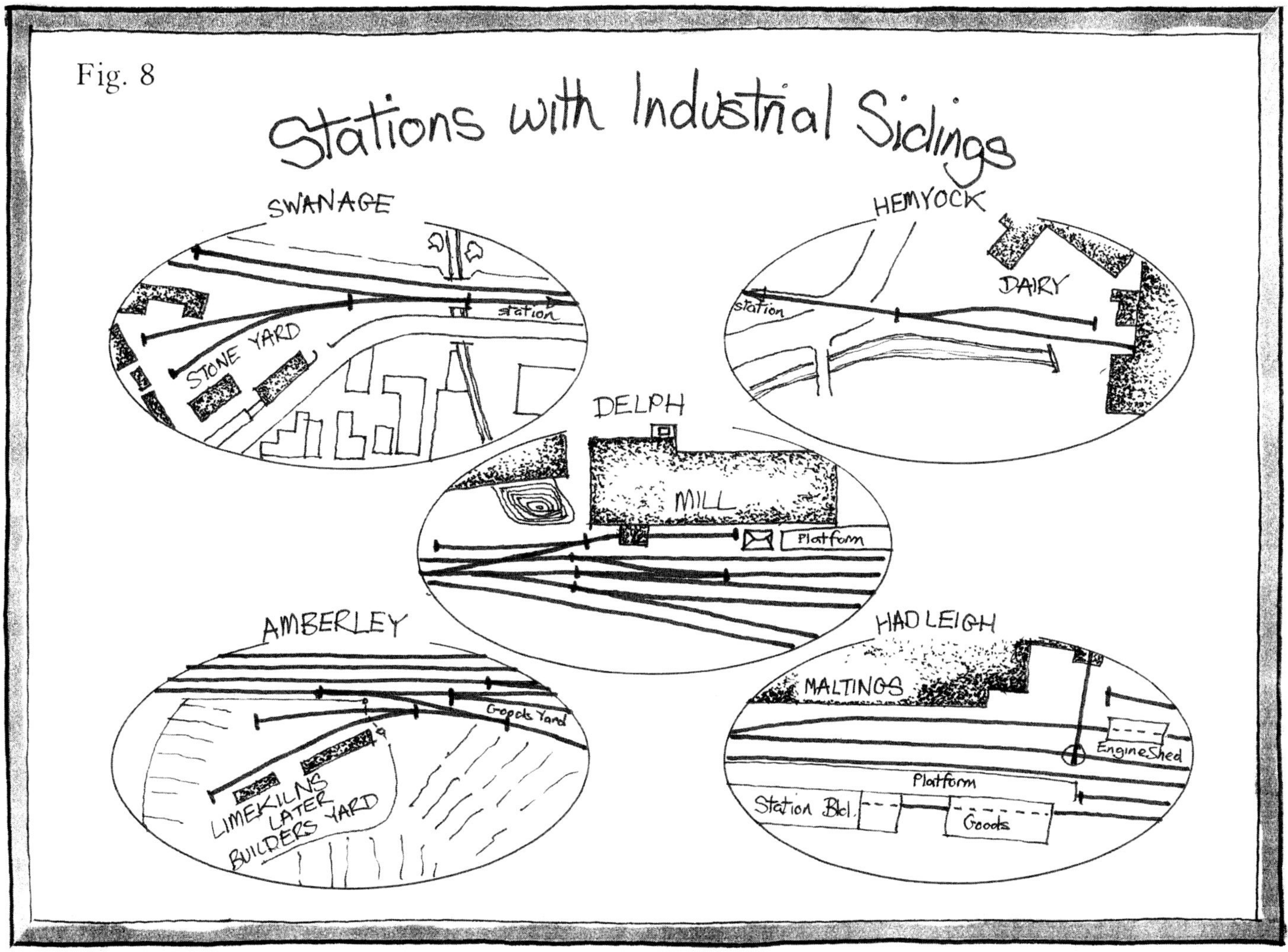

Stations with Industrial Sidings

SWANAGE
station
STONE YARD

HEMYOCK
station
DAIRY

DELPH
MILL
Platform

AMBERLEY
Goods Yard
LIMEKILNS LATER BUILDERS YARD

HADLEIGH
MALTINGS
Engine Shed
Platform
Station Bld.
Goods

Scenes like these reflect the endeavour of local people through centuries of day-to-day life. Locally found materials and traditional ways of doing things have given our towns and villages their own unique character. If this is reflected in our models we will begin to build layouts that seem part of the community they serve. These views of Great Missenden in 1939 and 1937 have much to tell us about a period in time and local individuality.
S. H. FREESE

Purbeck stone was cut and dressed. Likewise at Hemyock, a large creamery dominated the rural skyline. Sometimes, however, the railway connection was not so distinct, like the builders yard built in the exhausted chalk quarry at Amberley. There were many sites like this which could enrich the operation of your layout, so look out for them.

I have included several stations in which an industry inspired me to design a plan. Dolwyddlan (page 78) had an interesting slate wharf, to which I added a narrow gauge line. This helped to build up the Welsh nationality of the station as well as adding to operation. I have also made frequent use of private sidings slipping out of a station, like the gasworks at Wantage (page 79) and the quarry at Mytholme (page 72). These can broaden the variety of wagons and freight operation. Sometimes the impact of the industry may rather dominate the layout and form its main focus, like Ruspidge Colliery (page 80) or the Ironstone Railway at Charwelton (page 94). Occasionally a whole line relied for its existence on one industry, and clearly the design based upon Abergynolwyn (page 82) reflects the importance of slate quarrying to the Talyllyn Railway.

Increasingly, I hunt for a track layout that offers plenty of scope to run different types of trains. Interesting operation does not necessarily mean a complicated layout overflowing with sidings, but rather a choice of station in which quite different trains operate. The branch line passenger train meeting the express at a junction, or stone-laden wagons brought from a quarry to shunt in the goods yard, offer opportunities to make operation more worthwhile. Hallatrow is a good example of this (page 84). Stone was brought from a local quarry into the station and shunted into goods trains for its journey further afield. Similarly, the colliery at Camerton sent its output along the branch to the junction from where it could be sent to perhaps Bristol or Bath. One can only imagine the busy shunting engine shuffling wagons from siding to siding, marshalling trains for onward transit while passenger trains from Frome called at the station and then passed the assiduous scene. A prying eye may have also caught a glimpse of the branch railmotor in the bay after bringing in passengers for connecting trains to Bristol.

I also consider the landscape surrounding the station. Landscapes vary considerably throughout this country and I would like to think that I could stand by a layout, and get some idea of where it is supposed to be, just by looking at it. This is easy where the countryside is dramatic and characterful, but more difficult in those middle counties, like here in Northamptonshire where 'the County of Squires and Spires' offers less that is exciting and distinctive.

I am reminded of a very pleasant holiday spent in Hartington, where we walked the Tissington Trail and got to know the open and windswept peaks of Derbyshire. We found the scenery often bleak and stark, but always dramatic and invigorating – a good subject for a model. There the limestone walls weave a web over the faintly undulating countryside, enclosing and taming land that once lay free. It was a scene blessed with few trees, with only the occasional shelter belt or

The station (at Great Missenden) should remain the focus of a layout, but the perceptive modeller would be wise to consider the landscape and architectural style of the buildings bordering the railway. This will complement the trains that run, and help to establish the identity and character of the location. J. H. RUSSELL and H. E. SIMMONDS

copse softening the harsh landscape. A layout set here would have to capture some of this magic, and reflect the rugged attractiveness of the area.

This would contrast sharply with another of my favourite haunts – Suffolk. A flatter (some would say flat) landscape here spreads out in a sea of flowing corn, swaying from field to field in a seemingly endless drift towards the horizon. This is very much a managed landscape and one that man has constantly changed. The small fields, once crossed by reaper and bailer, have now disappeared to the huge appetite of the combine harvester as it cuts paths through acres of prairie. It is worth considering changes like this, as a model set just forty years ago would present a very different scene from that of today. The intimate small fields, and the hedges that divided them, and the magnificent elms that once graced the hedgerows, now killed by disease or felled by the modernising farmer, may all be reinstated in model form, recreating the flavour of the county in better days.

The buildings in any landscape tend to contribute to the unique character of a county. The hay barns of Derbyshire or the black and white cottages of Herefordshire are so typical of these areas that they must surely be included in a model. For this reason I find Suffolk an exciting county. I like the pink cottages with their plaster-clad timber frames, twisted like old men, sitting alone and with dignity within the landscape. This richness of architecture I find very appealing; give me, any day, the washed walls of sixteenth-century farm houses, the tiny flint and brick cottages, or the warm hues of pantiles against the never-ending blue sky on a summer's day.

In winter the scene is quite different, when sharp raw winds blow from the east, the golden fields of August having given way to the grey clouds of November. A few months later the delicate early spring buds will disappear into summer once more. Modelling a season is an interesting idea, and one that deserves to be explored. A whole model could be dressed in a style that is just a little more interesting than the layout next door.

Whether you choose the windmills of Norfolk, the cotton mills of Lancashire, or the oast houses of Kent, the character of the landscape surrounding the layout must be considered. It is also important to be aware of the changes that progress has made, so that it is not only the liveries of the locomotives or the age of the cars in the station forecourt that establish the period.

SPACE FOR A LAYOUT

If you think you haven't room for a layout, don't be disheartened; a layout can be built anywhere and to any size or shape (*Fig. 10*). Without the luxury of a railway room, an attractive model can be built into a showcase and displayed

Trussed timber-framed buildings, rendered with lime plaster, huddle beneath their pantiled roofs. All are different, each with its own individual story that we can only guess at. Humility like this should be observed and woven into the thoughts that we have about our modelling plans. This is Debenham, Suffolk, in 1946, and its character should shout from our model.

S. H. FREESE

within your home (*Fig. 11*). It is surprising what can be squeezed into a small space, as my plan of Wantage shows (page 79). By adding a couple of small fold-down fiddle yards, it would make a challenging shunting layout within an attractive model townscape.

A minimum space layout has become very popular of late. I have been very excited by John Spencer's light railway model he called Ruyton Road. This oozed atmosphere and yet was so small. John's model would not fit into a cabinet but could well be stored easily in the home, perhaps in a cupboard, perhaps under a bed. I have drawn my own version (page 86) that I have called Wellington Street Goods Station. This is

Ruyton Road, a fine example of using a small space without losing any of the layout's atmosphere, which, in this case, reflects a light railway in neglect. PHILIP HALL

How much space have you?

actually a near copy of a goods yard near Stockport which attracted me because of its large warehouse and the four-tracked viaduct behind the scene. I thought that not only could I use the front sidings as a goods loop on which to bring trains in and run round them, I could also display my excesses of stock high on the viaduct. It is a small layout that could fit any room, and one that could be changed in character by altering the buildings and scenery, as I have shown in Wellington Street (page 87).

A layout which has to fit along the wall of a room can easily prove too long, especially once the fiddle yard is added. This is why several of my plans are very small, like Dursley on page 88. To combat the problem of length, a bigger layout can be built by folding the track plan around a curve, and making it fit into the corner of a room. I designed Selsey for this location (*Fig. 12*) which, as you can see, fills a slim few feet either side of the corner (page 89). Pilton (page 92), the Lynton & Barnstaple Railway's main workshops, was made to fit a similar space and would make an interesting narrow gauge model.

Some people have the luxury of a spare room which can be dedicated to a layout. I chose a space of 9ft x 12ft as representative of a spare bedroom in a modern house. The room I am working in is just that size. My first idea was to fill it completely around the walls with a railway, as I have with Camelot (page 74) and Charwelton (page 94), but there are other ways. Building a circle in the middle of the room is an idea I developed with Abergynolwyn (page 82). I particularly like the way the line followed the natural contours of the hillside as it

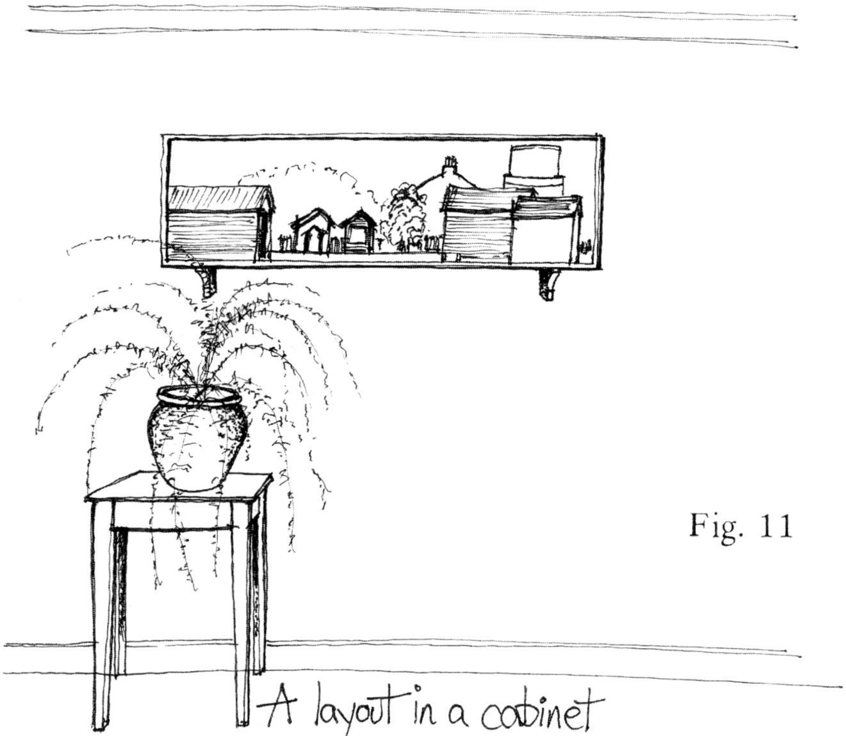

Fig. 11

A layout in a cabinet

Fig. 12

S SCALE

SELSEY

Placing a layout in the corner of a room

twisted and turned out of Abergynolwyn, passed beneath the winding drum and on towards Alltwyllt. In fact this layout, if stretched into a straight line, would be about 30ft long, yet it fits into our room, demonstrating how much can be gained even in this 7mm scale model, by making a layout circular.

Lyminge (page 96) is a rather unusual variation on this theme, combining two sites, the station and the junction at Harbledown. Operation could be very mixed with fiddle yard to fiddle yard services or a continual circuit, perhaps a test track. Running in a circle is also possible with the design based upon Rolvenden (page 100). However, here the layout is presented very differently — a large landscaped diorama. Although designed to 4mm scale, it could be modelled in 2mm, making a spectacular scenic layout.

Moving out of the house and into the garden is another possibility. A garden shed (*Fig. 13*) offers, in my view, far more flexibility than a room in our house. Of course, a large shed, say 12ft x 8ft, may be desirable, but I chose this small 8ft x 6ft shed to show just what can be achieved in such a tiny space. A shed bought from somewhere like an Argos Superstore is not very expensive, in my view offering an entirely practical way of making space for a layout. The beauty of a shed is the adaptability of its space and the possibility of going outside the four wooden walls. Very often in a model, the fiddle yard takes up much unnecessary space, but, with a layout in a shed, the fiddle yard can be placed outside the building in an enclosed and weatherproof box. My plan of Dornoch shows just this, and demonstrates how economically the space within a shed can be used. A wilder

Fig. 13

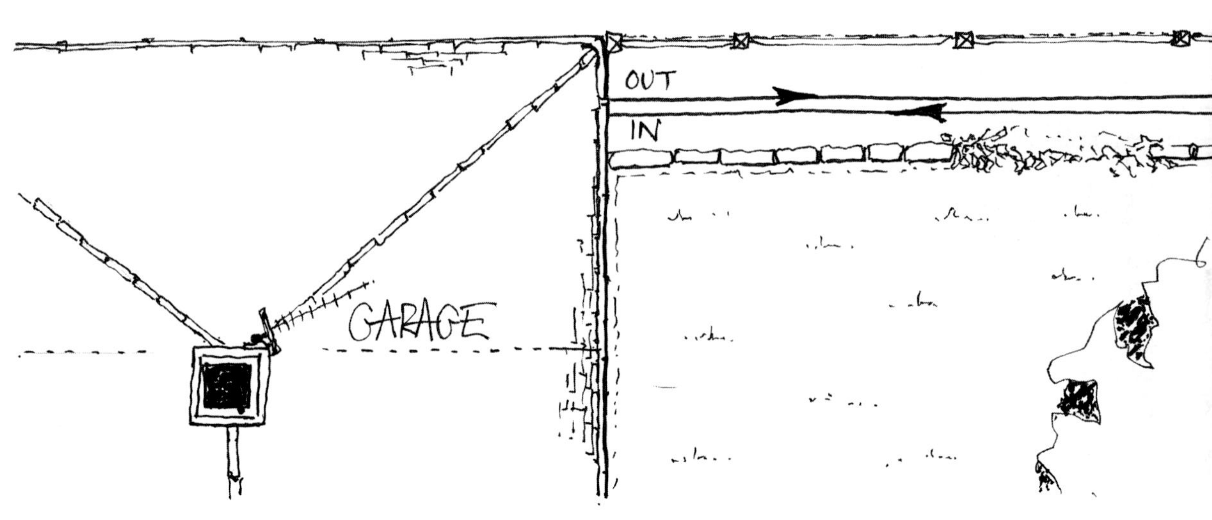

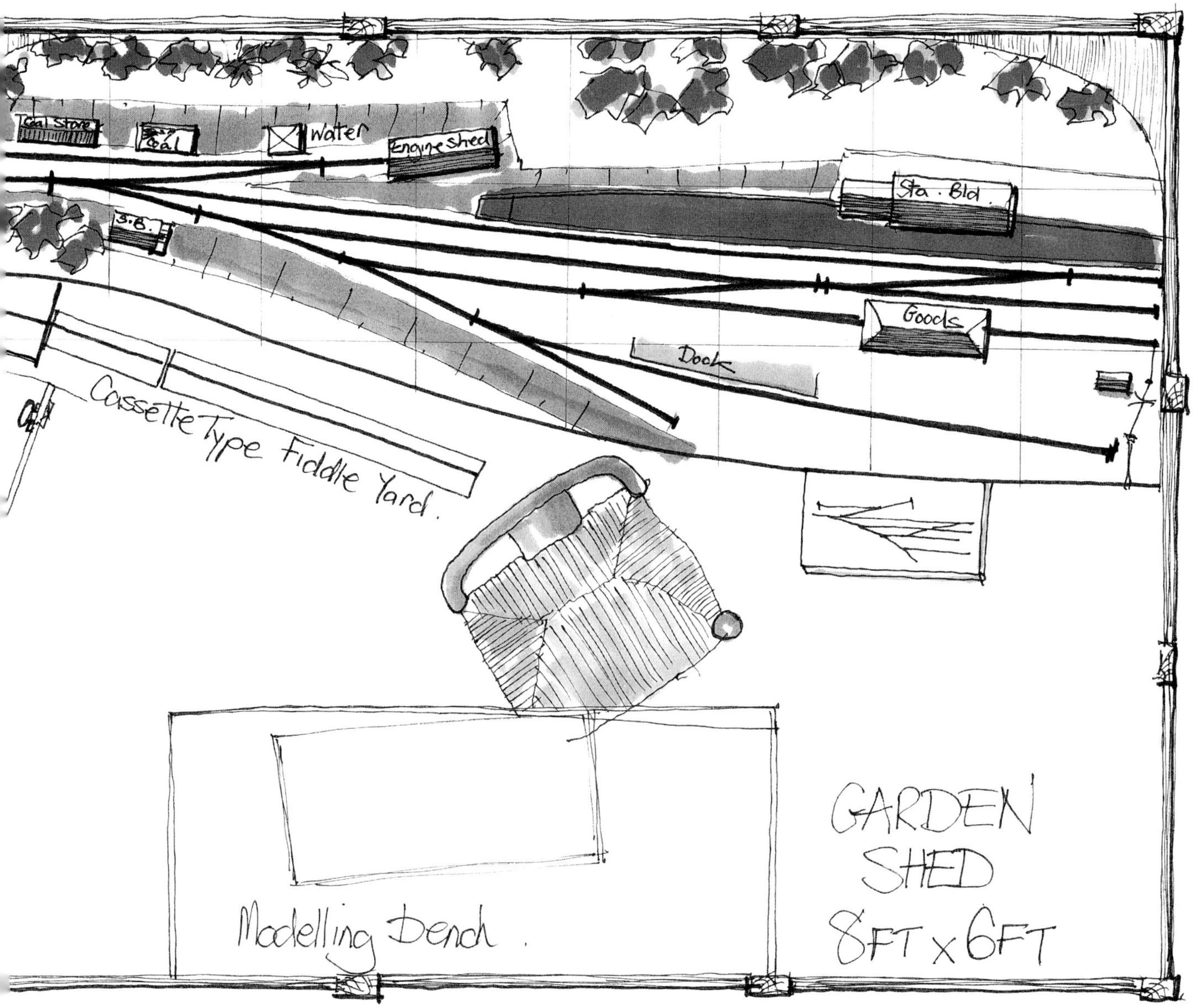

Coal Store
Coal
Water
Engine shed
Sta. Bld.
S.B.
Goods
Dock
Cassette Type Fiddle Yard.
Modelling Bench.
GARDEN SHED 8FT x 6FT

'O' GAUGE GARDEN LINE
GARDEN SHED 16FT x 6FT

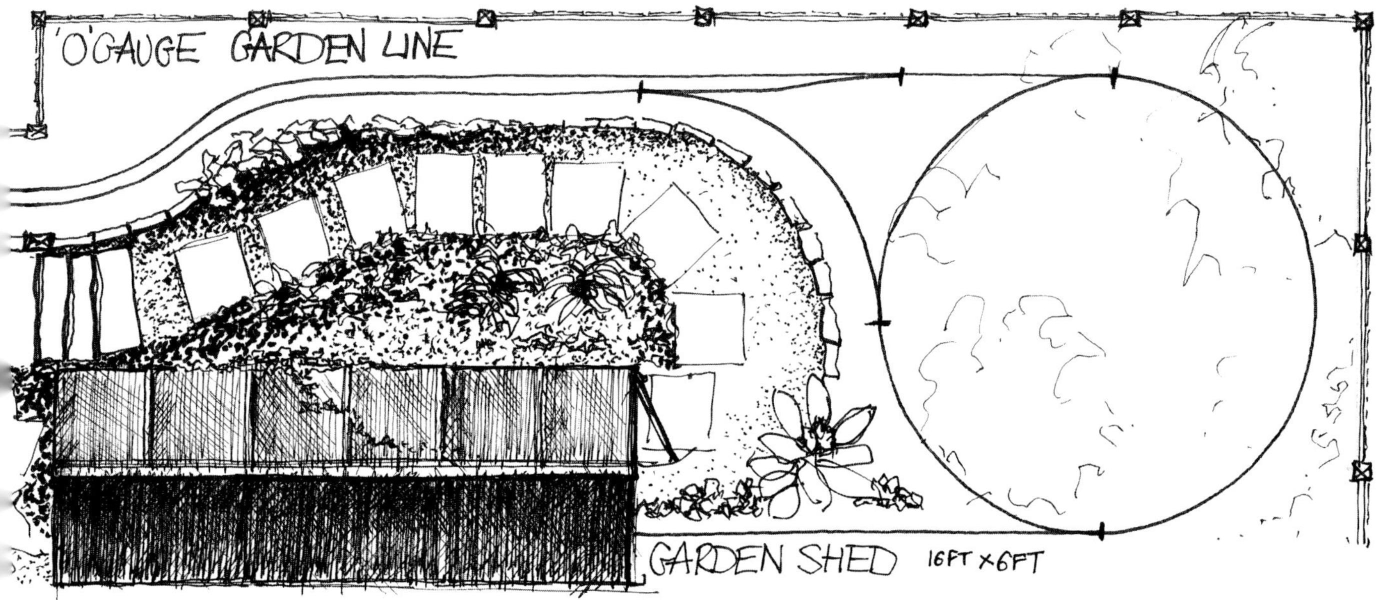

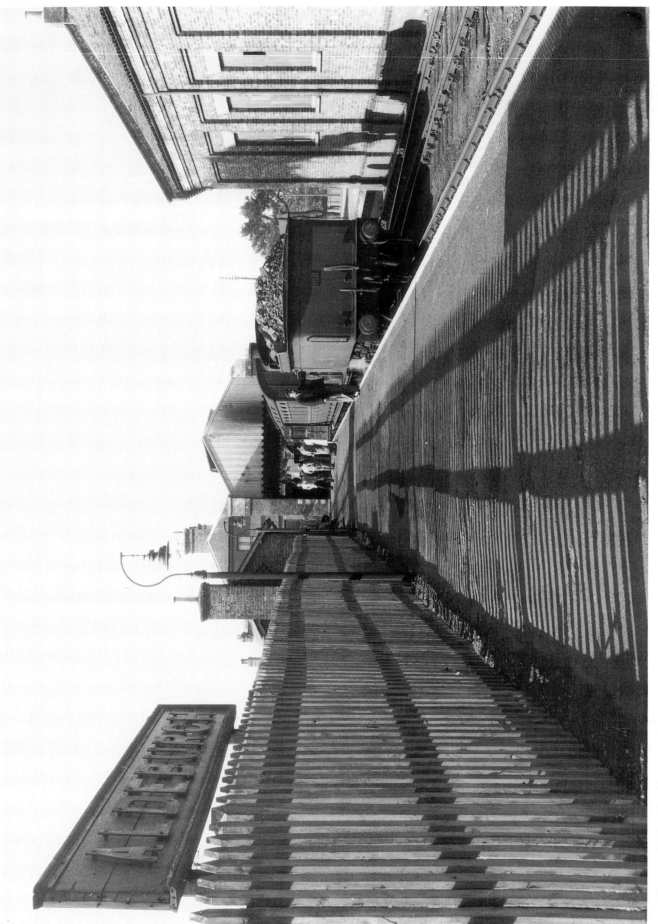

Photographs like this will start a collection from which a prototype plan can be developed into a design for a layout.

W. A. CAMWELL

idea is shown in the way I have adapted Tiviot Dale to this 8ft x 6ft shed (page 90). Here the rather wasteful curves (which always need disguising in some way) sweep out of the building and make their way round and under the layout to form a fiddle yard. Continuous running on a double-track main line is now a reality, using space that would not normally be available inside the house.

Overcoming the problems of confined space can prompt some imaginative consideration of our surroundings. I hope one of these suggestions might inspire further thought, and encourage you to find your own solution. We can now move on to the detailed planning of our proposed layout.

GATHERING INFORMATION

Before I start designing a layout, I need photographs and, as I have mentioned, a track plan to guide me.

Where do the prototype plans come from? A very accessible source is in the many books published by Wild Swan. The plan for Aldeburgh (*Fig. 14*) has been taken from *Great Eastern Railway Engine Sheds Part 2*, and it may be interesting to see how I have altered it in this design. Useful track plans can also be found within the pages of books published by Oxford Publishing Company, in addition to the many railway magazines available. However, for the more unusual, or if you have one particular pet scheme in mind, it may be a good idea to contact the British Museum, or County Records Office for copies of Ordnance Survey maps. The

Fig. 14

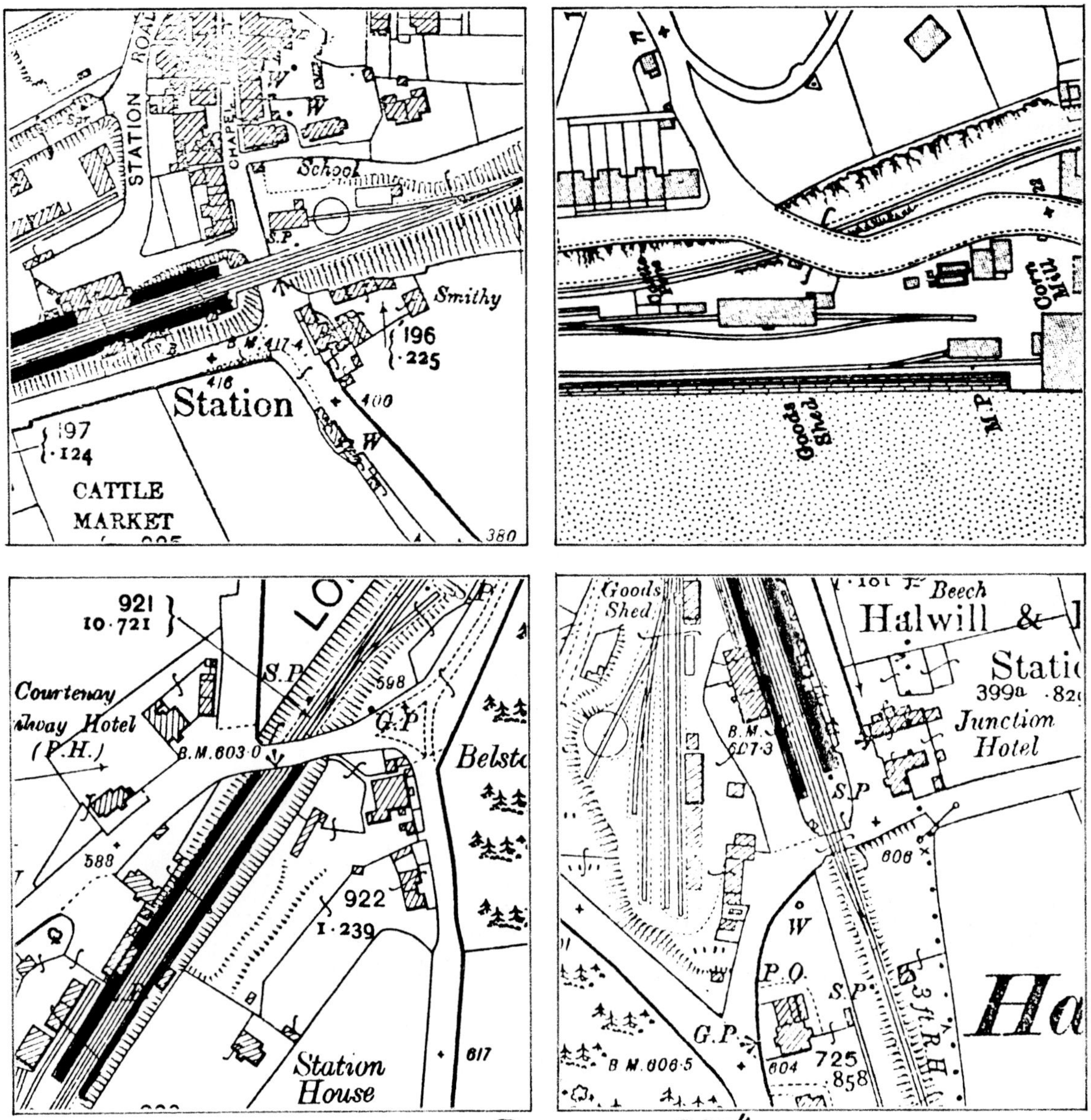

Fig. 15 Ordnance Survey 25" maps

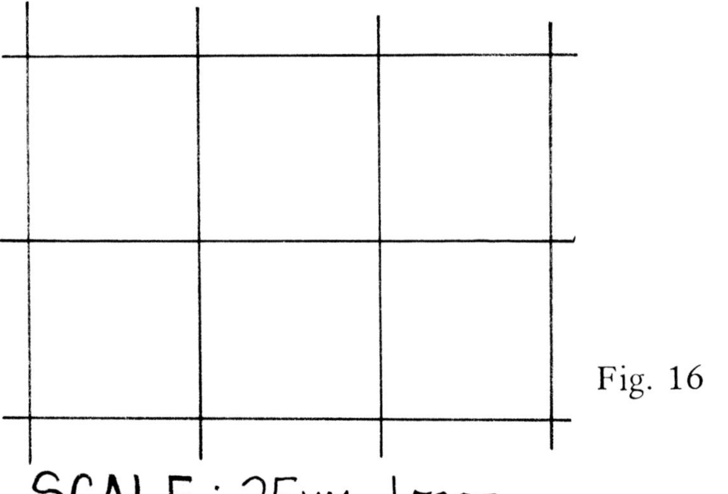

Fig. 16

most useful are the 25in scale which are available in a number of editions. Each edition represents the date of the survey, thus a Second Edition would be about 1907 (*Fig. 15*).

This investigative work can be rewarding and lead us along avenues that we may not normally tread. My association with the Aysgarth project has taken me to the Dales twice. We have walked the hillsides, taken many photographs and enjoyed ourselves in the fresh air, often discussing the fruits of our day's work over an evening meal at the Rowan Tree. It has also given me something to look for when I see a box of postcards at an exhibition, and has opened my eyes to the attractions of the North Eastern Railway.

DRAWING A TRACK PLAN

I like to draw with a 2B pencil, the softness of which makes it easier to sketch straight or flowing lines. I generally enlarge the station plan I'm interested in to a scale of 25mm equalling 1ft on the model (*Fig. 16*). I find this a nice size to work in, not too small and fiddly, yet not too large to draw comfortably. This enlargement may be done on a photocopier, but I usually do it by placing a gridded piece of tracing paper (with squares that represent 1 sq ft) over the plan.

With this master plan drawn, I can set about simplifying it and shortening it. I usually tape the master to a window and, by putting a thin piece of A3 paper over it, I can trace through the lines I want, cutting out bits, and sliding the plan around to draw the design. Although this makes my arms ache, it is easy to do, and I'm able to keep track of the prototype as I think my way around the plan.

The length of a layout can obviously be reduced by shortening sidings. This is an easy solution to the size problem, but care has to be taken to avoid making them ridiculously small. A siding that runs into a coal yard and only holds three or four wagons can look very unprototypical. It is much better to leave it out of the plan and have fewer, but longer sidings. A snip can also be taken out of platforms and bays without much worry, provided a train of respectable length can still stand alongside them (*Fig. 17*).

The appearance of trackwork, as it weaves and flows through a station, can be very attractive and can even motivate many people to choose a particular layout. Certainly there is something satisfyingly graceful about watching a train snaking its way through crossovers, slips and simple turnouts into a goods yard, and this is something that must not be lost in the design. With the pressure to save space, it may seem inviting to use short, tight radius turnouts, like A5s (approx 36in rad) – but stop! I would strongly guard against this as I feel the appearance of many a good layout has been spoilt by this false economy. It is better to use B6 (approx 54in rad) or B8 (approx 96in rad) turnouts, and reduce the length of the model by leaving some

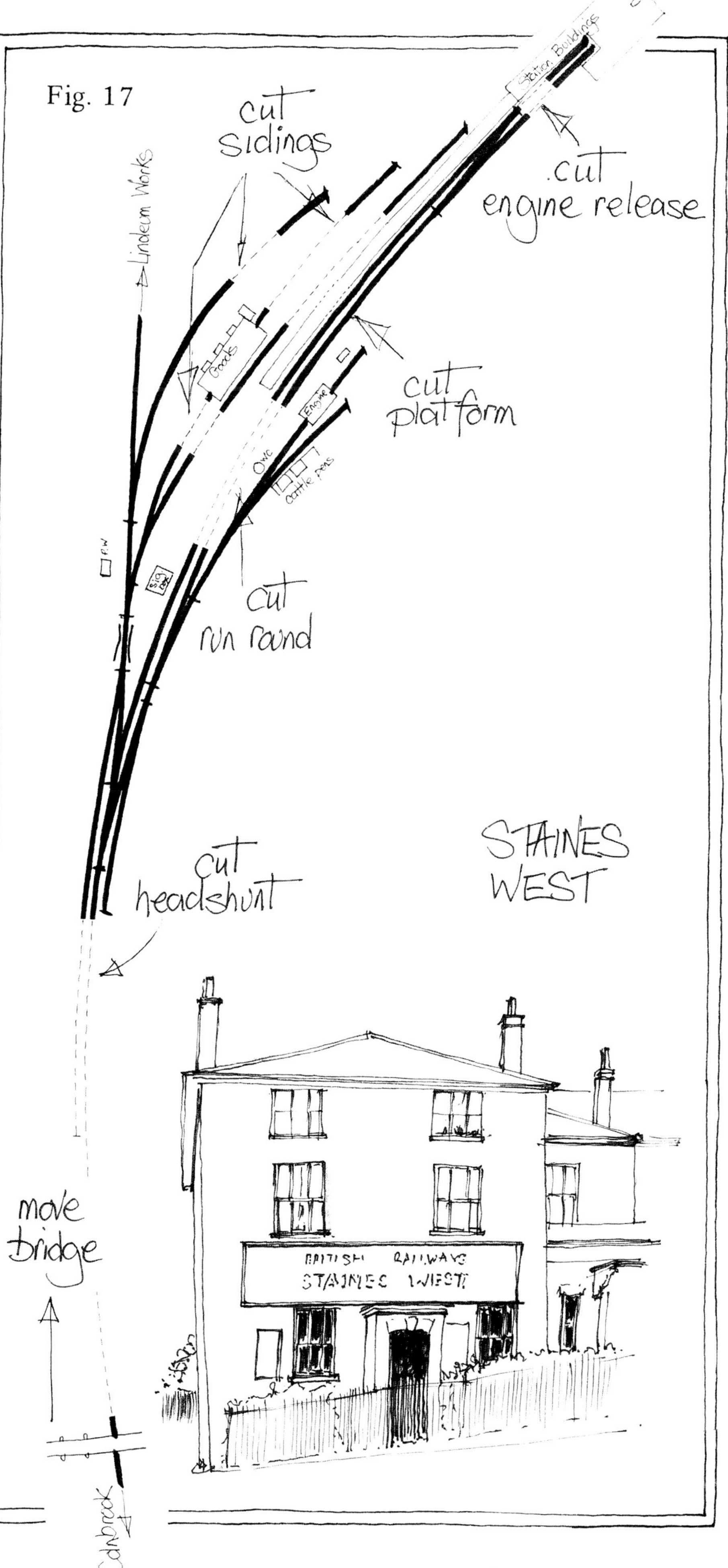

out altogether (*Fig. 18*). Very often it is possible to obtain the same operating potential by using a fiddle yard to complete the shunting manoeuvres. This idea was used, as mentioned, with 'Lydham Heath' but also on both high and low sections of 'Inkerman Street' (*Fig. 19*).

CONSIDERING A FIDDLE YARD

Probably the simplest form of fiddle yard is the sector plate. This swings a single length of track from siding to siding (*Fig. 20*) and can be used to shunt trains and/or direct them to some kind of storage sidings. It is an idea I have incorporated in many of my designs. It has many merits and enables us to run round an arriving train and then shunt (as in the case of my Wellington Street Goods design on page 86) without the complexity and spaciousness of pointwork or the space required for a lengthy run-round loop. Alternatively, the moving track featured in my Dornoch design (page 21) directs trains to the storage sidings which I have arranged in the form of track units, in the Chris Pendlenton tradition. These storage roads could well be a fan of sidings (Abergynolwyn, page 82) or a set of parallel lines like the ones I have hidden under R. A. Lister's factory at Dursley (page 88).

There are many different types of fiddle yards, and it is worth pondering over which one would be suitable for your particular circumstances. *Fig. 21a* is a simple swinging yard (like that used with 'Inkerman Street') onto which trains can be driven and swung from track to track. As any line can be used for this purpose, it doesn't matter which one is left empty. *Fig. 21b* is similar, the difference being the moving of the pivot to the centre of the yard. Whilst it is still possible to shunt from track to track in the same way, it is also possible to turn the whole unit around and reverse the direction of the trains. I found this particularly useful when I operated 'Petherick' at exhibitions. There simply wasn't enough time to uncouple an engine from an incoming train, lift it to the other end and drive it out onto the layout again. This also saves handling the stock. It is often called the 'Denny fiddle yard' after the man who developed it – Peter Denny. The next type (*Fig. 21c*) rolls backwards and forward and can also be shunted upon. However, I feel that this is the most difficult type to construct and make it slide smoothly. The most recent design (*Fig. 21d*) was invented by Chris Pendlenton and has become very popular. Each section of track, or 'cassette', is separated and can be shuffled around to compose the type of train that is needed.

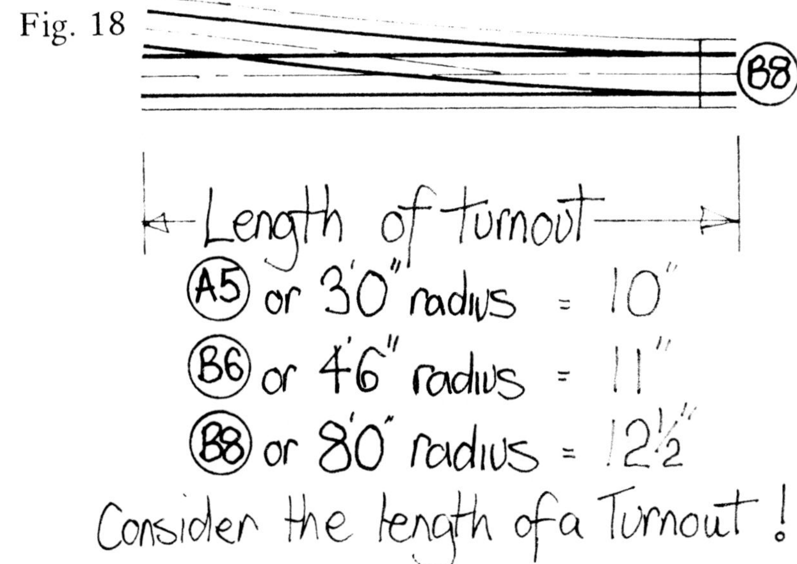

Fig. 18

Fig. 19

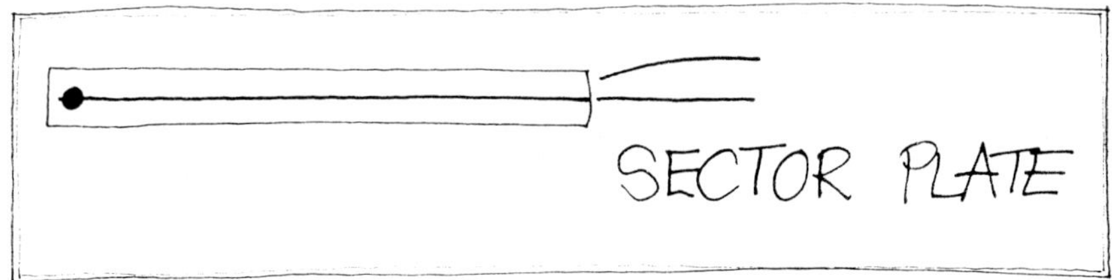

Fig. 20

The short sections hold one locomotive, whilst the longer strips hold a train. These can be used in conjunction with a vertical rack, on which spare sections are kept. This is a very simple system, but not, I feel, as slick to use as a pivoted yard. Design *Fig. 21e* is perhaps self-explanatory, and to my mind has only one disadvantage – the amount of space lost due to the turnouts, making it a very long fiddle yard. A development of this type is *Fig. 21f* in which the last 12 inches (long enough for a locomotive) is pivoted so that an engine can be shunted from one end to the other without lifting it.

I have used different types of fiddle yard in various of my designs. A swinging yard (*Fig. 21a*) becomes useful in the designs at Mytholme (page 72), Alnwick (page 77) and Aldeburgh (page 98), enabling the completion of shunting manoeuvres, whereas a fan of sidings (*Fig. 21e*) appears more appropriate in

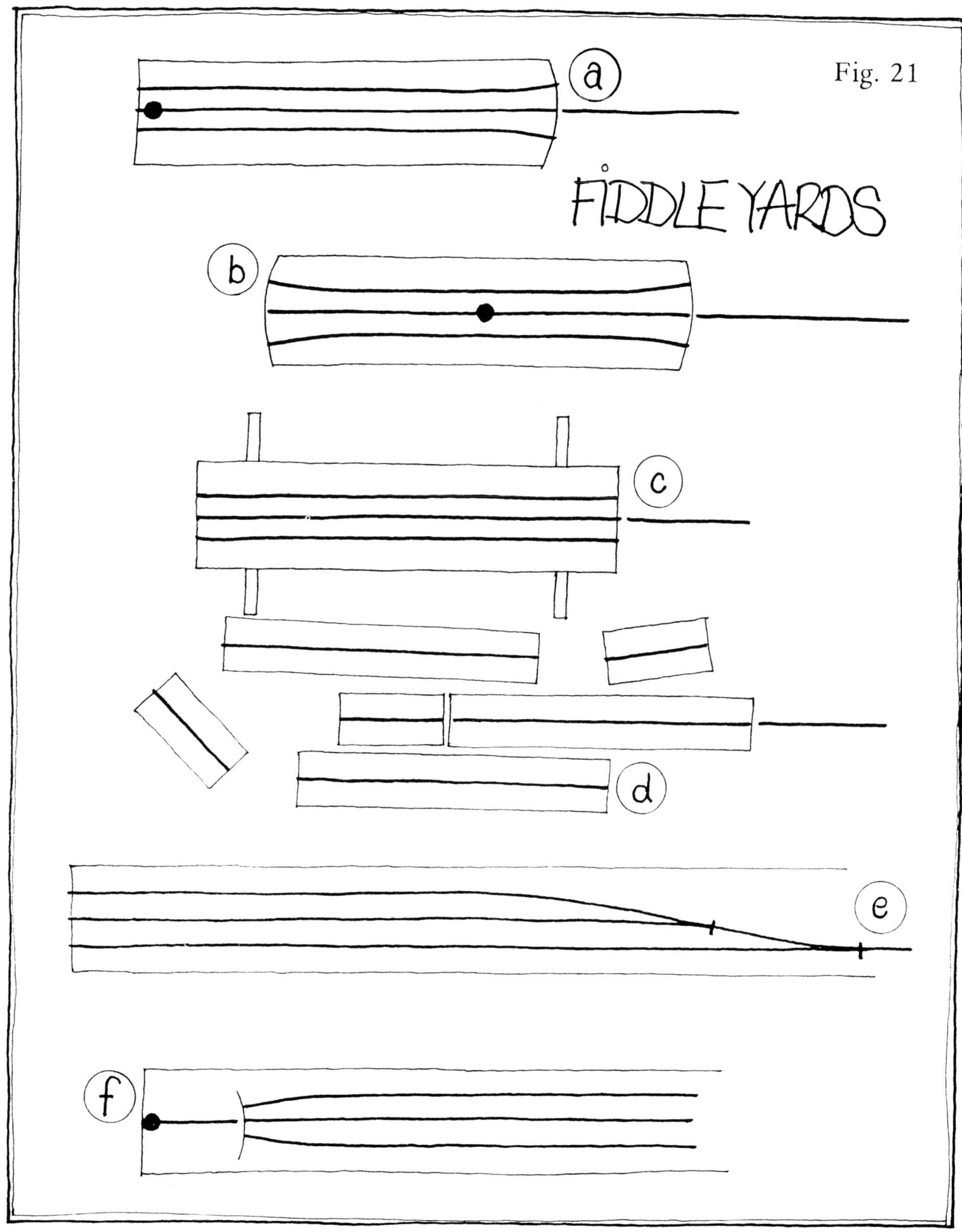

the plans of Rolvenden, Charwelton and Tiviot Dale. It is now time for you to decide how you would like to operate your layout so that you can select the most appropriate type of hidden sidings.

Once I feel I have completed this task, I look again at the track plan and carefully review it, making very sure I haven't shortened any turnouts (*Fig. 22*) and checking that the sidings and platforms are of respectable length. Sometimes it may be necessary to do this several times, until I get the design I want. I may well alter the whole plan, perhaps by putting the layout on a curve that wasn't present in the prototype.

When I'm finally satisfied with the track plan, I add the platforms, station buildings, signal box and other railway buildings. These will be the bones of the layout, but the flesh (the landscape around them) must also be carefully considered.

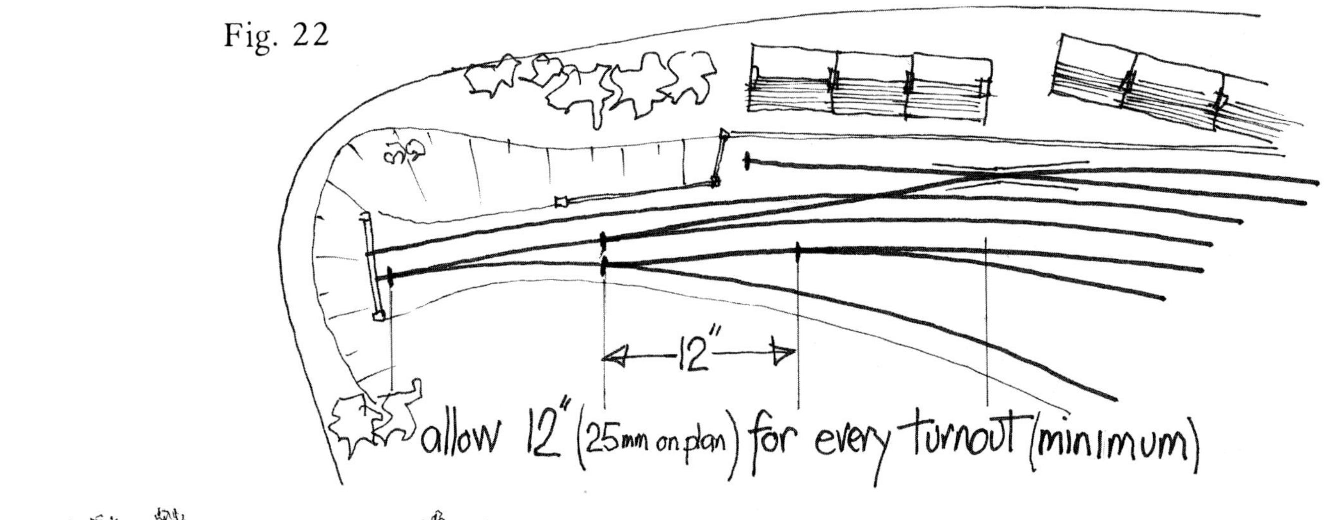

Fig. 22

COMPOSING THE LANDSCAPE

We have discussed the ways in which a fiddle yard or sector plate can be used to store and shunt trains from siding to siding. Clearly we do not want to draw attention to this, and need to find a scenic way of disguising it. Visually there are many things we could do.

Traditionally the choice has been between a tunnel (*Fig. 23*) and an over bridge that spans a cutting (*Fig. 24*). Whilst these solve the problem quite effectively, it may not be desirable to use either of these solutions on our particular layout. If I were to model an East Anglian scene, the flattish Suffolk landscape would not normally lend itself to a tunnel or, for that matter, necessarily a bridge over a cutting. However, it was common practice to raise a road on earth banks to lift it over the railway (*Fig. 25*) and so this solution would not look out of place (consider Aldeburgh, page 98). Alternatively, some kind of viewing block could be created. I use trees frequently to achieve this, placing a group of perhaps three to break the viewer's gaze. The same approach can be adapted to a layout in which the track leaves the station on an embankment (*Fig. 26*). Here the

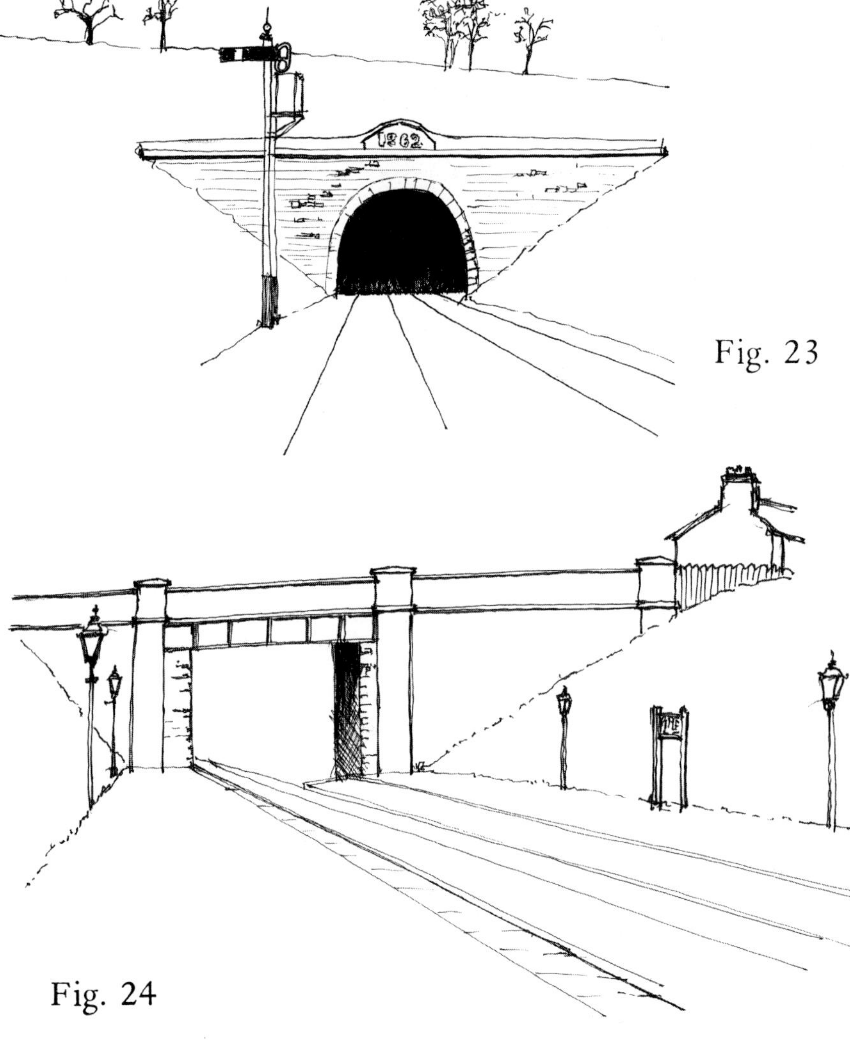

Fig. 23

Fig. 24

Fig. 25

Using a bridge in a flat Landscape

Fig. 26

Using trees to screen the end

A building can also be used

Fig. 27

height of the trees can be increased so that they overshadow the departing trains. The trees could be replaced with a building (*Fig. 27*). A woollen mill could be a useful structure for this, and I have placed one to block the exit of trains over the river and road bridges at Tiviot Dale (page 90). It is an ideally large building, but others, like the maltings at Bury St. Edmunds, could serve the same purpose. Here, the double-tracked line left the station on an embankment, crossed a road and then slid behind the brick-built maltings – consider carefully the location of your model.

A thoughtfully placed cottage, like the one in *Fig. 28*, would help to screen the disappearing train, and would also guide the eye over the level crossing, and towards the church tower beyond. The church could be clad in flint and the cottage washed in Suffolk pink, thus firmly establishing the environment of

Fig. 28

A building is used again to screen a train

the model. Buildings feature as viewing blocks in many of my designs. The engine shed at Selsey (page 89) was deliberately placed at the front left-hand edge of the design so that it would screen the line to Selsey Beach and any shunting manoeuvres into the goods yard. Similarly the engine sheds at Wantage (page 79) achieve the same result. A more extreme example of this idea is shown at Dursley (page 88) where R. A. Lister's factory dominates one end of the model.

Trees, bridges, buildings, even a simple cutting (*Fig. 29*) or carefully placed hoarding (*Fig. 30*) would disguise the departing trains and form the limits of a diorama. It is important to consider quite carefully how you can most appropriately solve this problem. Thoughtful planning will lead to a more successful layout.

Another issue that needs to be considered quite carefully is the backscene. Somehow the scene has to disappear without the far baseboard edge being noticed. On Petherick, the hills behind the station rolled down to the track and very successfully framed the layout, the hills met the sky at the horizon and the background melted into the scene. Clearly the attraction of Lydham was the

Fig. 29

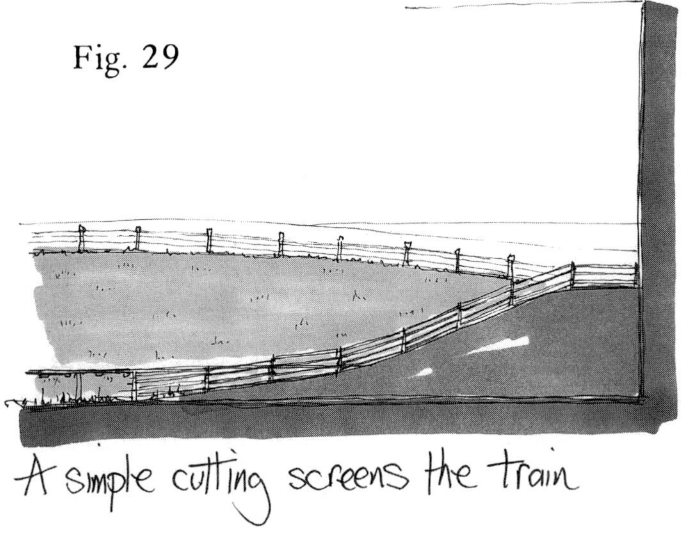

A simple cutting screens the train

Using a hoarding

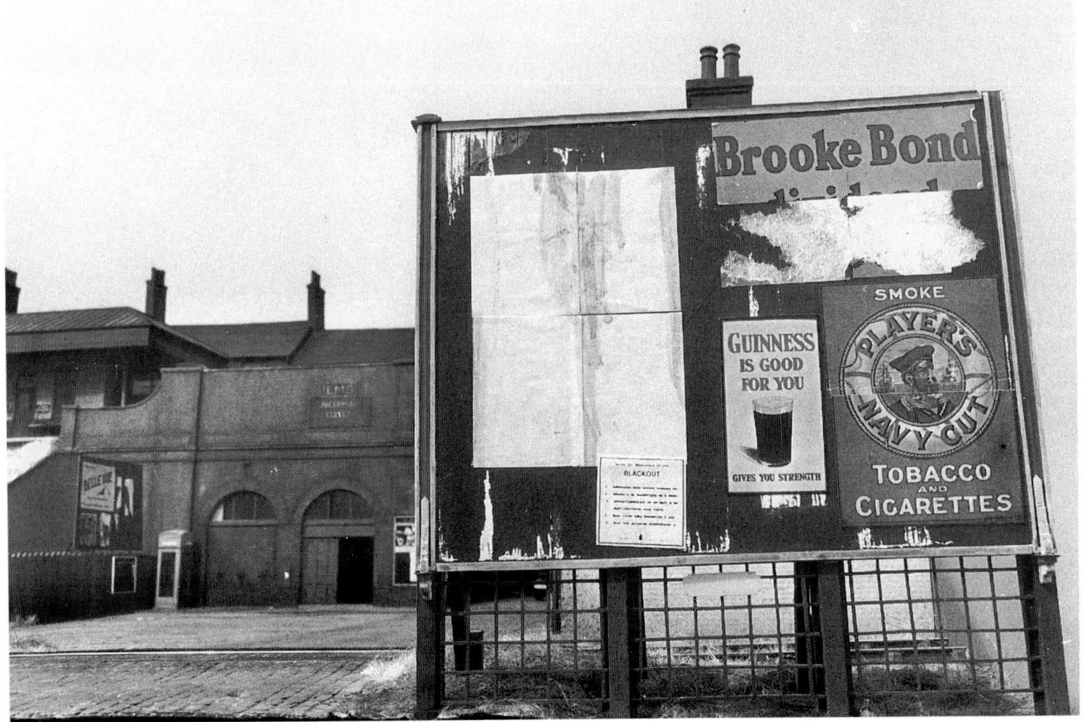

Something as simple as a hoarding not only makes an effective screen to departing trains, but, as this fine example by Bob Barlow shows, an opportunity to enjoy some imaginative modelling (Inkerman Street, 1990).

pine plantation, which very easily contained the eye, whilst at Inkerman Street, Moss Hey Mill and the red-bricked terrace houses solved this problem.

Ideally, the background should be higher than the foreground, so that the scene appears to slide away into the distance (the only exception to this would be a model that looked out to sea). There are many ways of doing this. I may look for deep retaining walls (as at Thorneywood in Nottingham) to keep the eye firmly on the model, or use the backs of buildings to create a similar effect. However, frequently the solution need be little more than a carefully placed hedge, perhaps slightly smaller in scale to emphasise the impression of perspective.

The nature of this background join between the sky and the ground, is an issue to which I feel much thought needs

Consideration needs to be given to what goes on in the background of a layout, so that we focus firmly on the model and away from the far baseboard edge. Height is an important factor and these photographs of Darlington Bank Top and Bishops Stortford show the usefulness of walls and buildings.

J. H. VENN and NATIONAL RAILWAY MUSEUM

I chose a hedge to disguise the baseboard edge at the end of Lydham Heath.

to be given. I often find, when photographing someone else's layout, that the lack of a convincing skyline presents me with many problems (*Fig. 31*). When I am trying to compose a realistic picture, I look at track level across the model and an undisguised edge will be very noticeable and spoil the illusion I am trying to create. Sometimes I may push wagons in front of it, but, if thought had been given to this in the planning stage, far more opportunities would have been opened up for the photographer. Try to imagine the view down the track at Lydham without the distant hedge that borders the lane. I included this and extended the end of the layout beyond the buffer stops, so this kind of view would look realistic.

What we are trying to achieve is a natural looking background within the minimum amount of space. Our problem perhaps starts with the way in which we view our layouts. We know that the horizon (the distant line that divides the sky from the ground) will always appear at our eye level, unless the land is hilly and rises above us. If we were to lie on a beach, then stand, and finally climb a cliff to look out to sea, the horizon would always appear to be at our eye level. This

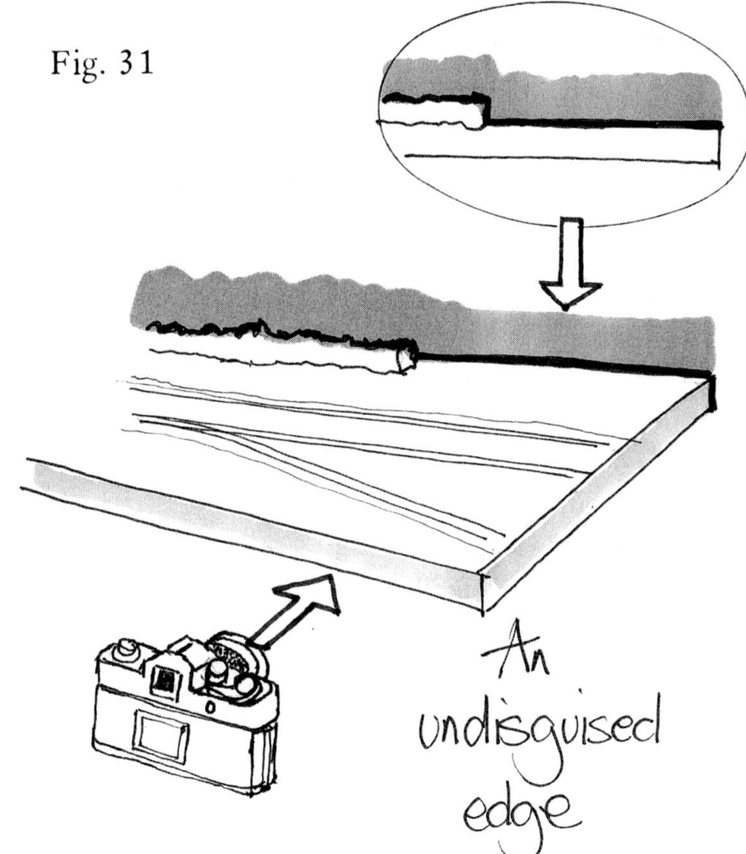

Fig. 31

Fig. 32

Fig. 33

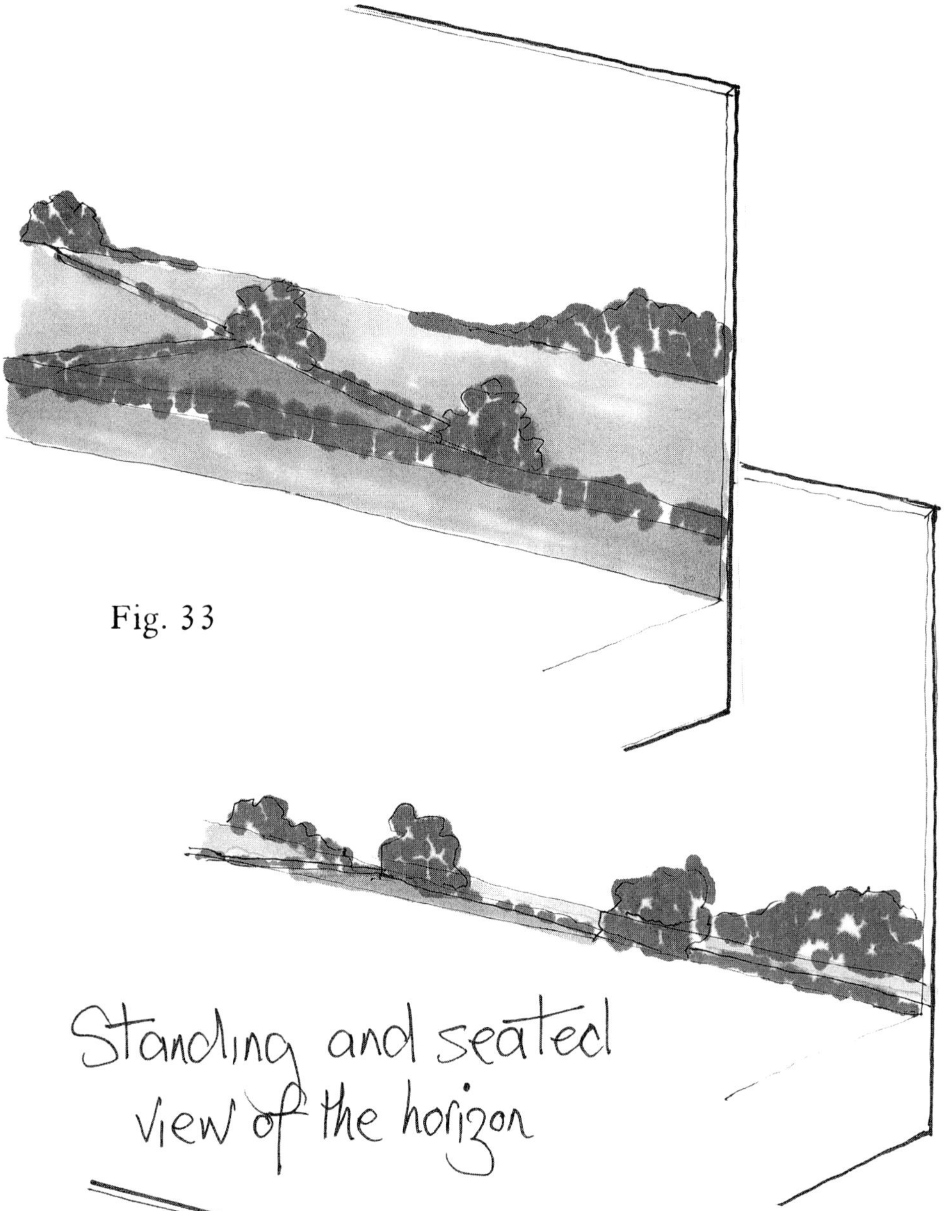

Standing and seated view of the horizon

Fig. 34

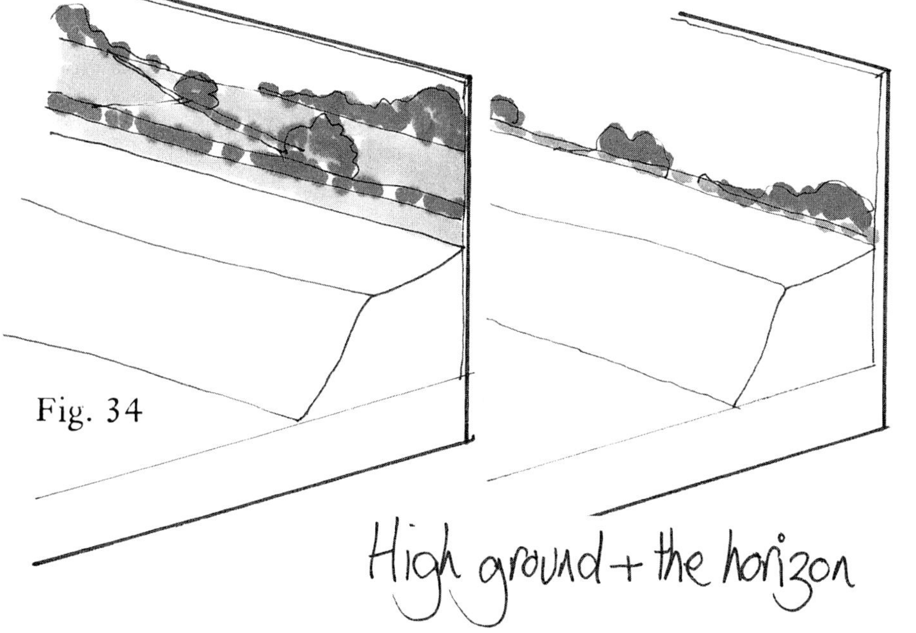

High ground + the horizon

presents a problem when three people of different height (*Fig. 32*) view our layout, as we can only model the horizon from one viewpoint. Similarly, if we stand up, we may expect to see the horizon higher (*Fig. 33a*) than if we sit down (*Fig. 33b*). If, however, the land behind the railway rises, this modelling dilemma is less evident (*Fig. 34*). Perhaps if you mentally remove the embankment in the lower illustration and imagine a painted background, you will see what I mean.

It is perhaps logical that we should look for a prototype in which the background is high. This takes us back to the point about the trees behind Lydham Heath, the mill behind Inkerman Street and the hills behind Petherick. Many prototypes do offer a useful and natural solution to this problem. The hillside falling down to the track and then continuing to the stream would make Rotherfield (*Fig. 35*) a good choice (see plan for Mytholme, page 72). Likewise, a similar but less spacious solution can be found at Hitchin (*Fig. 36*) where the chalk cliff maintains height but reduces width. In a similar way I have used a rock cliff or cuttings in my designs for Abergynolwyn (page 82) and Dolwyddelan (page 78) to keep the layouts narrow.

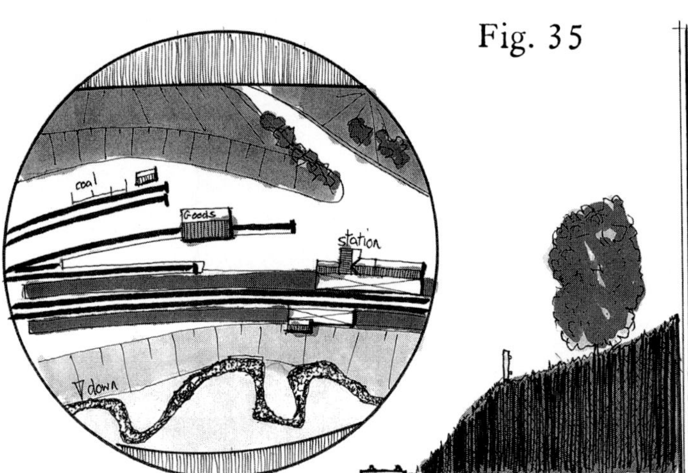

Fig. 35

High ground at Rotherfield

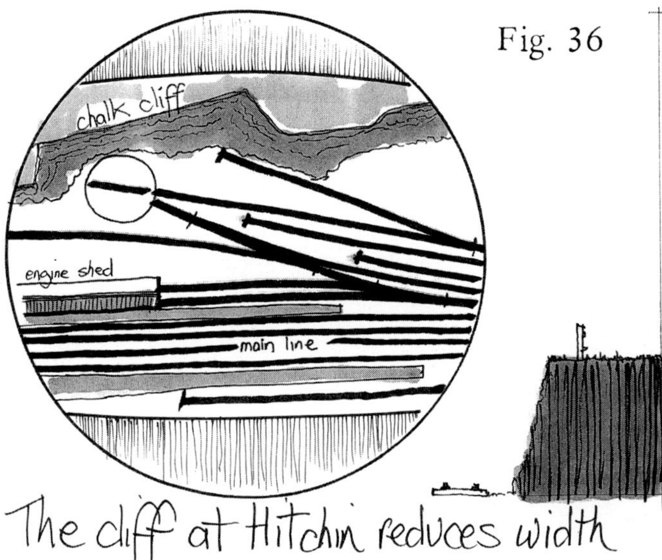

Fig. 36

The cliff at Hitchin reduces width

In little more than a shelf's width, the sea wall scene at Pendon has a convincing backdrop from a sensitively modelled cliff. A. E. SMITH

The sprawl of this motive power depot at Machynlleth is conveniently contained by the rock cutting behind it, an idea we could apply to other situations. B. M. BARBER

Equally convenient is this chalk cliff beside the Great Western main line at Pangbourne. A model would need but a few inches to reflect this very natural feature. L & GRP

Retaining walls are blended with a cutting in this view of Small Heath, Birmingham, which also shows common housebacks in the background. NATIONAL RAILWAY MUSEUM

Retaining walls need not only be found in towns and cities, as this view of Coalport shows. Note also the steepness of the embankment and the overshadowing trees, which, combined with the buildings behind, provide a rising backdrop. This marvellous photograph is also full of other inspiring ideas, like the back yards and washing hung from lines neighbouring a warehouse that would make an ideal viewing block to trains departing to a fiddle yard.

Fig. 37

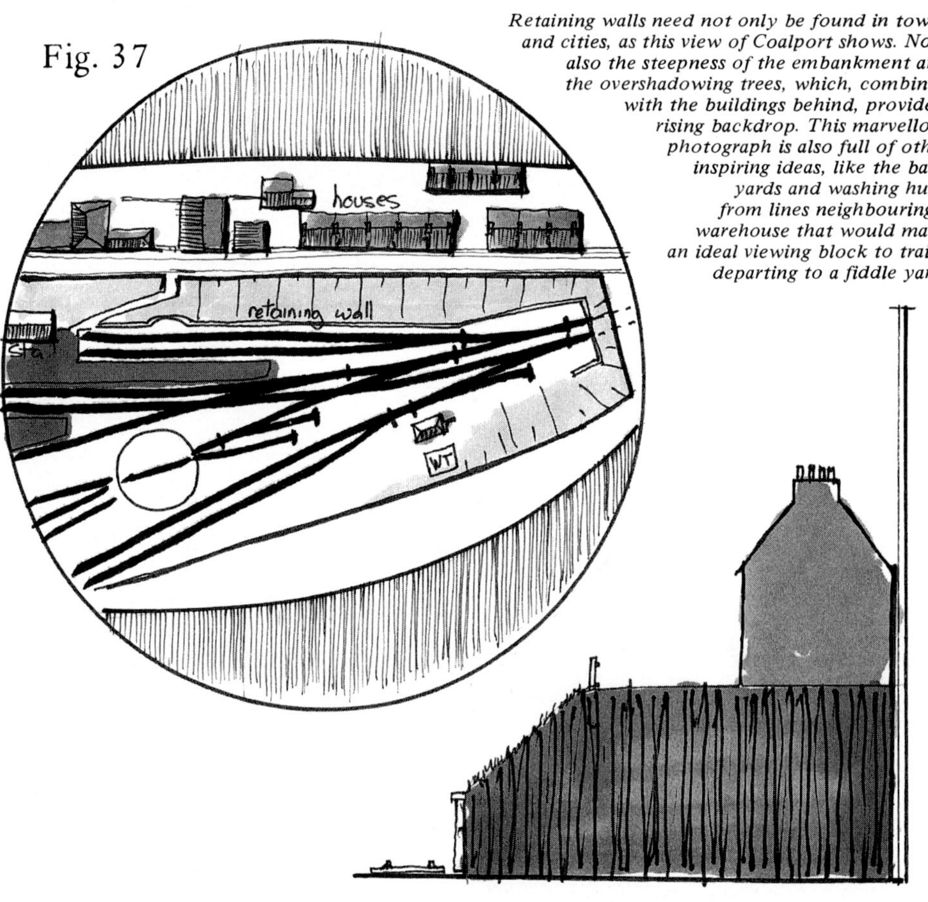

Retaining walls, embankment and buildings

The effect of a cliff on a model is equal to that of a retaining wall – it saves space. However, it is often possible to combine a retaining wall with an embankment, as a kind of halfway-house measure. Sometimes this could be topped with buildings (*Fig. 37*) as the illustration of Hibble Road shows. This combination is quite ideal as the building creates much height and removes the need for a painted scene. Other prototypes feature buildings close to the railway fence, a well-known example is the group of warehouses that stand behind the goods yard at Ashburton (*Fig. 38*). My designs for Redruth (page 81) and Chisledon (page 102) explore the placing of buildings to hide the horizon, whilst Dursley (page 88) makes excellent use of half relief (modelling half a building) to create an industrial atmosphere in very little space.

Buildings overlooking a railway should be looked out for, to see how well they can be used to close the scene. W. POTTER

C. L. MOWAT

Warehouses at Ashburton. J. H. MOSS

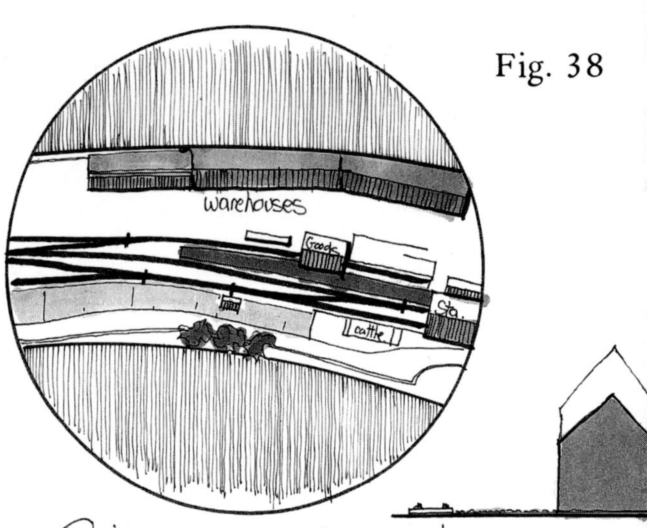

Buildings used as a backdrop

As the line divides, the girder bridge and stone embankment become both a raised backdrop and a screen for some hidden sidings. The buildings fill in the background but could be brought forward along the street, adding character, interest and detail to the scene, which is believed to have been at Swansea.

This tightly packed shed scene at Longhedge in 1938 opens into the multiple tracks of the Southern main line, yet closes with warehousing that could be modelled as towering half relief shells just a few centimetres deep. H. F. WHEELLER

With this much detail in so small a space, the careful use of half-relief building would make this intimate scene at Birmingham in 1941 ideal in 7mm scale. NATIONAL RAILWAY MUSEUM

Chris Pendlenton used buildings of various architectural styles to form a background to his North Shields layout.
CHRIS PENDLENTON

Some stations are overshadowed by woodland, and I have chosen Dornock (*Fig. 39*) in the Highlands of Scotland to exemplify this. I will make little comment about the time and tedium it takes to make all the trees, but I will say that all the effort is well rewarded by the result. Perhaps one of the most awkward of landscapes to convincingly portray must be the flattish countryside in East Anglia. We have mentioned the height of buildings and a maltings would do very nicely. However, this is not the answer for every station, so we have to make do with something much simpler. I favour breaking the far edge of a model with a hedgerow and perhaps adding (to create interest) a copse of trees as with the drawing of Swaffham Prior in Cambridgeshire (*Fig. 40*) which must rate as one of the flattest parts of this country.

We might also consider perspective whereby as we look across a landscape, the distant trees, hedges and buildings appear smaller than those in the

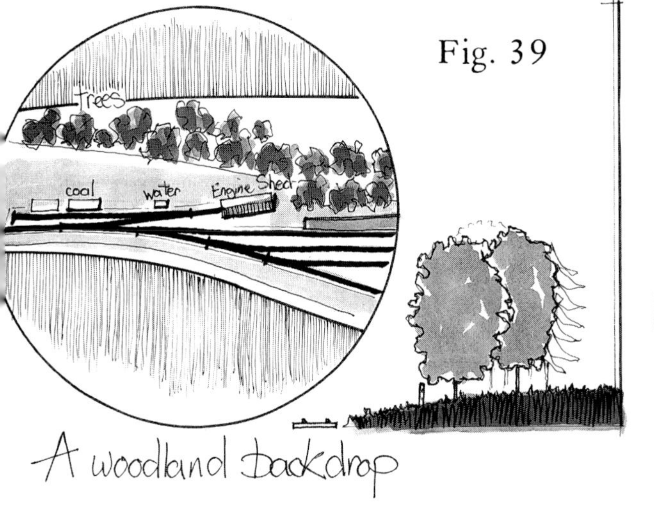

Fig. 39

A woodland backdrop

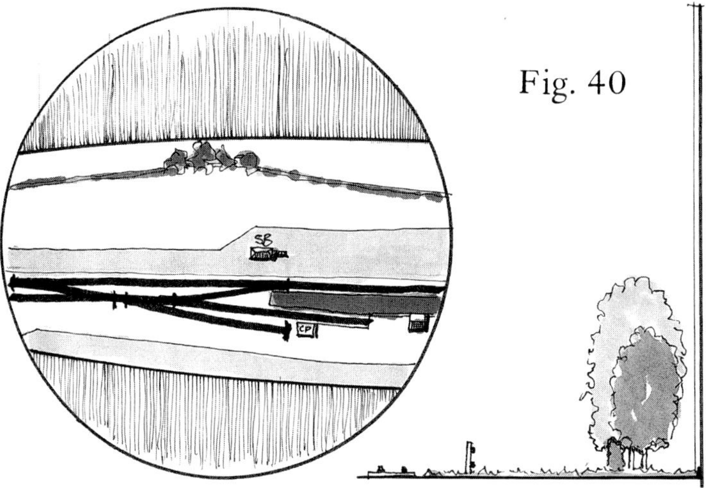

Fig. 40

A flat scene broken by a hedge + trees

This mid-Suffolk scene on John Watson's model of Kenton, carefully blends the model landscape with the backscene by thoughtfully placing hedges near to where they meet.

The careful reduction in scale and detail of the buildings in the background helped to create a greater illusion of depth to Copenhagen Fields.

foreground (*Figs. 41 & 42b*). We can use this effect to suggest distance in our models by deliberately reducing the scale of distant hedges, trees and buildings (*Fig. 43*). If done carefully (making them smaller than they should be in scale and proportion to one another) the effect can be surprisingly convincing (*Fig. 44*). If smaller features are grouped closer together, we have, in effect, been able to squeeze more background into a smaller space. Even though we have distorted it in reality, the scene should look natural. Even exaggerating the slope of a hillside (*Fig. 45*) will look alright provided we don't view our layout from the side. If hedges and buildings are kept parallel to the front edge of the layout, the changes in scale will not notice much (*Fig. 42a*).

The landscape surrounding the railway becomes increasingly important in 2mm scale, and provides an excellent vehicle in which to experiment with perspective modelling.

Fig. 41

When
the scale is
reduced – view from front

Fig. 42a

Fig. 42b

As this flat Mid Suffolk landscape recedes into the distance, our eye level remains firmly with the horizon. It is low to the ground and would only appear to rise if we stood on or climbed something to lift us higher, so that we begin to look down onto the scene. Mid Suffolk Light Railway.

S. H. FREESE

As is apparent in this photograph of the level crossing at Biddenden on the Kent & East Sussex Railway, distant trees very quickly appear smaller than those in the foreground. This is the effect perspective creates in a scene. In our models we can deliberately reduce the scale of these far trees, which will allow us to bring them closer to the near trees, yet maintain a realistic appearance, and save space. R. K. COPE

Fig. 43

Fig. 44

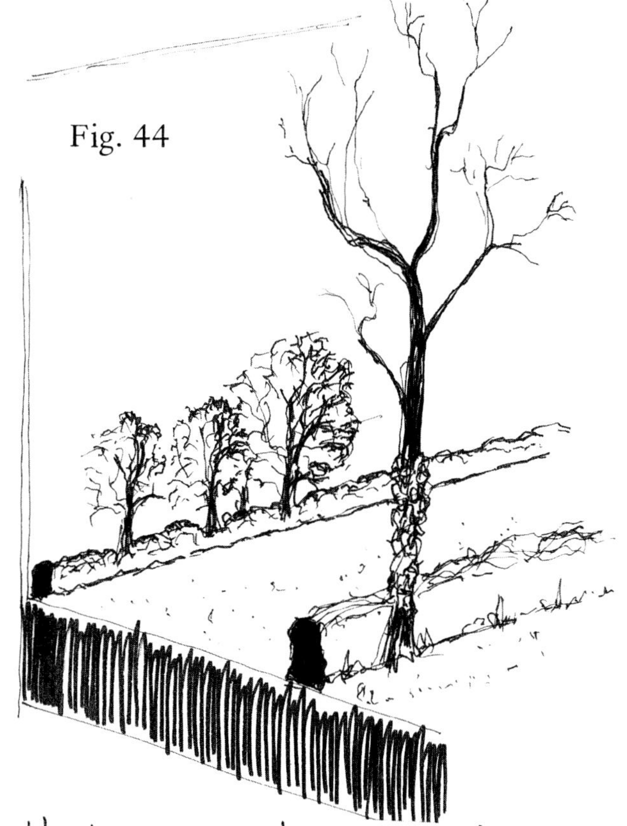

Hedges can be moved nearer,
when their scale is reduced

High ground behind a model can be dramatic in helping to present a natural and imposing scene. A small amount of painted backscene complements the sensitive modelling of the Peak District landscape surrounding Chee Tor.

Fig. 45

Exaggerate the slope of a hillside

By exaggerating the slope of a hillside, more can be squeezed into a small space. However, it is advisable to gaze on it only from its intended viewpoint – the front.

To reflect the rolling hillside surrounding Ashburton, John Birkett-Smith successfully mixed a painted backscene with a modelled background.

The disappearing effect of perspective is more dramatically seen when looking down a lane. The sides appear to converge as they approach the horizon and the height of hedges appears to get smaller (*Fig. 46*) – this is known as one point perspective. All lines appear to vanish towards one point, a principle we can use successfully on our models, with some limitations.

We could start simply by narrowing a lane, progressively reducing the height of the hedges, and perhaps folding the line of our view until it is parallel to the backscene (*Fig. 47*). However, a more challenging problem could be the perspective modelling of a road between houses

Fig. 46

The effect of one point perspective

Fig. 47

Reduce width of Lane

This magnificent view of Bierton Road, Aylesbury in 1938, spells out all we need to know about perspective. The horizon is at our eye level, the telegraph poles appear to get smaller and closer together as they fade into the distance, and the lane seems to narrow as it winds towards the next village.
S. H. FREESE

Find the vanishing point (eye level) and trace the building lines disappearing towards it, then consider how some thoughtful modelling could compress this scene at Cambridge Street, Aylesbury, in 1944. S. H. FREESE

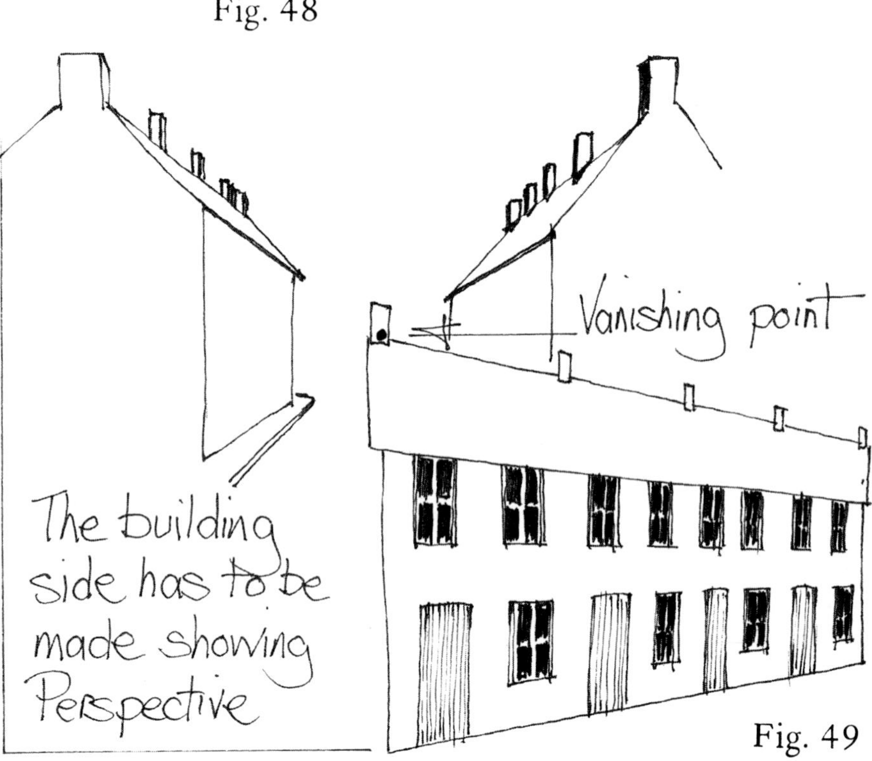

(*Fig. 48*). If we look down the road an look up at the buildings, we have t consider more widely the effect o perspective. If we were to model thes buildings out of card, the sides woul have to be drawn and made in perspectiv (*Fig. 49*). This means that the horizonta parallel lines, like the top and bottom o windows and the ridge tiles, woul disappear towards one point. Also, eac building (if it were a terrace) woul become narrower than its neighbour Whilst this emphasises perspective, an allows us to squeeze a lot in a small space we would have to block a sideways viev of the road.

There is much to play with; we coul explore the effect of two point perspectiv (*Fig. 50*). The disappearing of lines to couple of vanishing points fixed on th horizon would enable us to reduce th scale of a building near the back of th layout. Its sides would appear to ge smaller the further they were away from us and we could exaggerate this. However we would have to be thoughtful in th way we modelled it and remember tha the horizon controls our view of th

Fig. 50

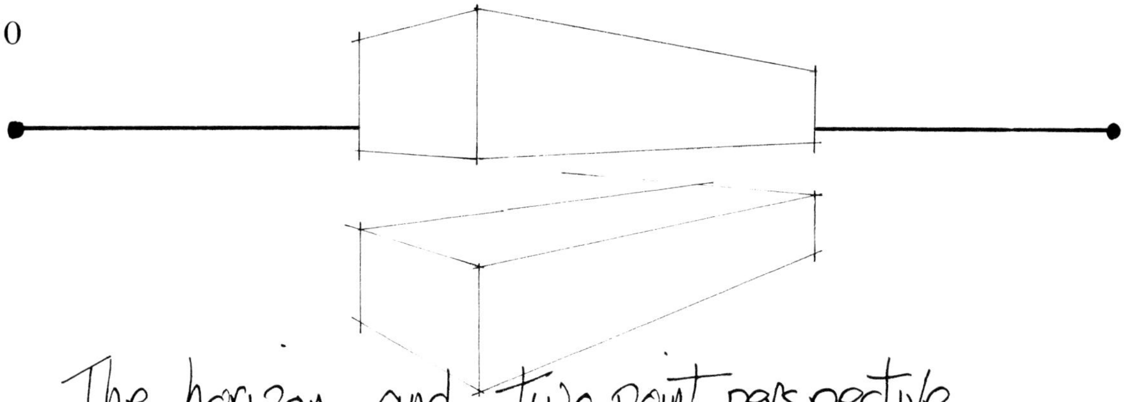

The horizon and two point perspective

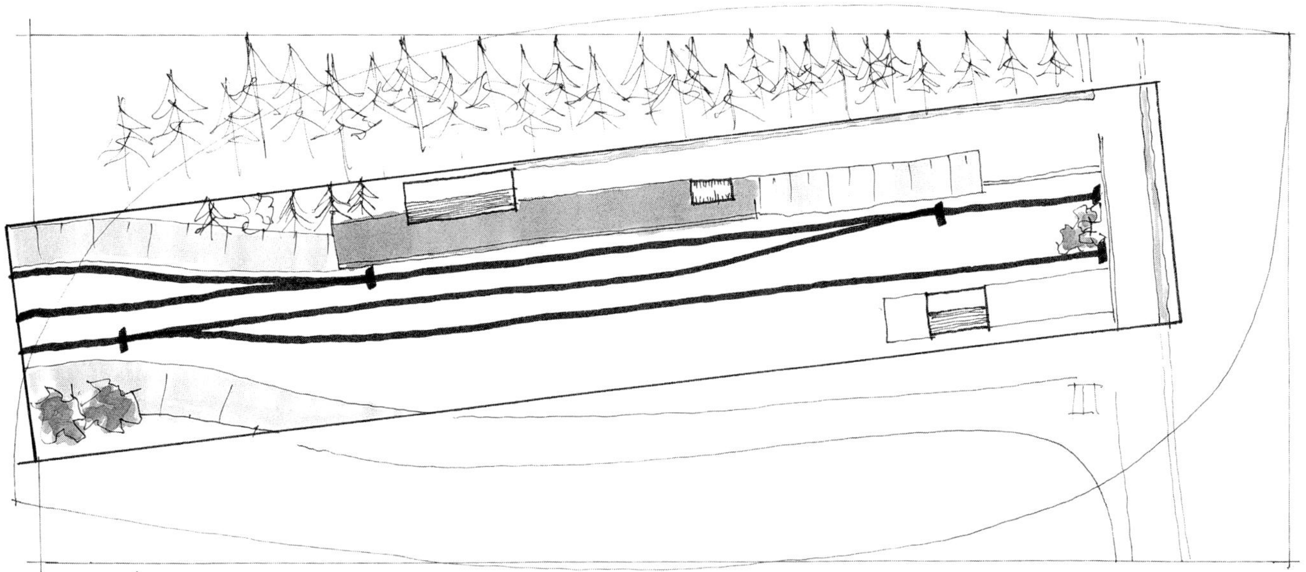

Consider the overall appearance of the layout, particularly its shape

Fig. 51

layout. If we stand too high, the distortions we have created would begin to notice – so be discreet.

The use of perspective as a space saver is worth pursuing. It allows us to create the illusion of depth through 3-D modelling and would be very useful in my plans of Tiviot Dale (page 90) and Rolvenden (Page 100). I would prefer to model as much of the background as possible and keep any landscape painting to a minimum (*Fig. 52*).

Fig. 52

Keep any painted backscene to the minimum

The simplest of backscenes are the most effective, as this prototype shot shows. A Metropolitan Railway 'H' class carrying its LNER number 6418, near Little Missenden in 1938.
S. H. FREESE

In my book *Landscape Modelling*, I thought that a painted backscene was a good solution to this problem, but I am now not so sure. I feel that few of us have the ability to paint it convincingly, and poor ones show up badly in a photograph. I would therefore suggest that painted backscenes are best left alone. If you feel like tackling one, I suggest you keep it very simple – perhaps just a wash of distant hills to suggest the line of the horizon. The exception that proves the rule must be Tom Harland's painted backscene to 'Bramblewick'. This is perhaps the most successful attempt I have ever seen – but Tom is an artist!

It is wise not to lose track of your vision, and perhaps now is the time to review what has been achieved so far. We did this many times when we were building Inkerman Street. We questioned what we should include in the model to capture the dullness of a rationed wartime urban community. We came up with Mr. Levine's builders yard, Mrs. O'Dell's corner shop, Omdurman Row, the blackened Moss Hey New Mill, and the stone-blocked forecourt to the upstairs station. However, it is vital not only to choose the right buildings and scenic features to set the scene, but also to place them on the layout in a meaningful and interesting manner.

On 'Petherick' I deliberately placed lanes so that the view along them would lead the eye to something really quite interesting. I remember that the view down one lane would show the station building with, perhaps, a train sitting by the platform, and the other would lead you through a farm gate to the signal box. When I photograph a model, I'm always looking for these shots. It is nice to catch a glimpse of a carriage door through the booking office doorway, or the smokebox of an engine between the ends of two buildings, or under the boughs of an overhanging autumnal tree. How nice it was, on 'Inkerman Street', to catch a tantalizing view of Mr. Levine's three-wheeler in the back yards of Omdurman Row whilst the washing from No. 4 hung lifeless in the still air.

The planning of the landscape may be developed further by deliberately placing objects in the foreground to obscure the observer's view of the more important scenes behind. Then he or she would have to look around them, being forced to see unexpected views, which might lead to a few surprises. This is why a train arriving at Petherick would be hidden in a deep cutting, before bursting under an overbridge, only to be partly hidden behind a cornfield before disappearing behind trees and reappearing in full view on an embankment.

When putting detail into a layout, I always feel that it is better to view the model as a series of interconnected scenes. It is more effective to concentrate detail into small scenes or cameos rather than spread it out widely over the landscape.

As I write this, I have in my mind a picture of Gordon Gravett's beautiful 'Ditchling Green'. This layout shows to great effect what can be achieved by working in a larger scale, and in particular the opportunity for including lots and lots of detail.

Similarly, Hursley bustled with interest and showed how powerful a larger scale can be in displaying detail – I particularly liked the interior of the engine shed, modelled as if the fitter had just left his spanners to unwrap his corned beef sandwiches from their grease-

A restrained and subtle wash of colour with a distant hint of detail, this is a masterly backscene behind Bramblewick. Tom's fine use of colour and choice of a sea view maintains a discreet backcloth to the layout.

The mixing of photographs with half relief buildings can be very convincing, as this view of Steve Hall's Halifax King Cross shows.

proof paper, before going to the signa box to get his enamelled mug topped up with tea. Everyday scenes like this can be placed meaningfully around your layout Deciding what they should be rests with the limits of your own imagination. I would, however, guard against the twee – like the traction engine in a corner of a field or the lengths of rail in a goods yar – look at photographs and see wha actually happened. Equally, there are nc rules about where to put interesting scenes, although, to some extent, the prototype limits what can be done, as i does tend to break down the model into interesting cameos – the station building goods shed, signal box, engine shed o overbridge. These can then form the focus of small scenes into which detai can be built, thus creating interesting

Buildings help to focus a scene by organising and dictating a certain viewpoint from the onlooker. This can be structured to create surprise and interest within the layout.
GEOFF KENT

A signal can become the subject of a cameo around which detail can be concentrated. It is better to focus detail rather than let it sprawl indiscriminately across the layout. CHRIS PENDLENTON

areas within the whole completed model. In this way the eye tends to travel from scene to scene and the model appears to have some purpose.

REVIEWING THE DESIGN

As the layout design comes together, it is wise to look beyond the detail and consider the overall appearance of the model and address the question of balance. It would have been very easy for me to have cut 'Lydham Heath' down to a very narrow width, especially as it was supposed to be a minimum space layout, but what would it have looked like? If I had removed the forest and the meadow in the foreground, it would still have been Lydham, but not in the way I had intended. I could have included the same buildings, the Bishops Castle Railway rolling stock, and the same track plan, but I can't say it would have conveyed the atmosphere that I was trying to capture. To me, the sheep grazing in a meadow and the dappled sunlight playing through the branches of Scots pines, were vital to the model.

It may seem simple enough just to widen a very narrow layout. I tried this with Lydham but the impression it gave was rather uncomfortable and proportionally unattractive. As I sketched the baseboards over the plan, the whole design began to look more attractive if the edges of the layout were curved. I particularly wanted to arrange the model so that it could be viewed from one end, as well as from the front, and I found that by curving the edges, I could remove the unsightly front corner and make the layout look much better (*Fig. 51*). In all the designs I have worked upon since, flowing curves feature quite prominently. I feel this is a more imaginative approach and one that gives a result more pleasing to look at. Very often a sweeping curve folds the back-scene around the model, by taking away the square corners, and this can be balanced with a gracefully flowing line at the front.

I believe that with thoughtful planning, a more creative model will evolve, which will keep the spark of inspiration alive so that the motivation to finish the layout will not be lost.

So here we are, a completed plan, and how it is presented is a matter of taste and style. There is nothing wrong with it left in pencil, but, for a more professional finish, black fineliners like the Staedtler Mars graphic liner are ideal. I use 0.5mm and 0.1mm pens for most lines, except the trackwork, which is heavier (*Fig. 53*).

MORE DETAILED PLANNING

If we are to go ahead with building the layout, it might be wise to draw a more detailed plan. From the original design it is possible to get a fair idea of what the

Fig. 53

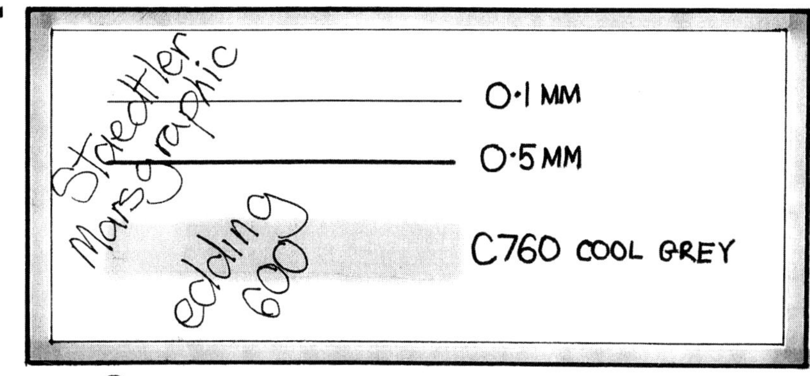

Pens used to draw plans

final layout will look like. However, the scale is small (approximately 1/12th full size) and this limits the accuracy of the drawing. By enlarging it, one could see more clearly, for example, the difference that using an A5 or B8 turnout would make. Similarly, it would be possible to assess more precisely the capacity of each siding, loop or platform (*Fig. 54*).

To make this next stage very easy, I have drawn and included within these pages, a collection of templates. These are drawn one-quarter full size (75mm to 1ft) and will help to produce a detailed working drawing in a manageable scale. They include left and right-handed turnouts, Y turnouts, diamond crossings, single and double slips, all to three different crossing angles and hence different radii. These should allow you to produce a huge combination of track formations (*Fig. 55*) and, in combination with the plain and curved track templates (*Fig. 56*), plan your whole design. As a bonus, I thought it would be useful to be

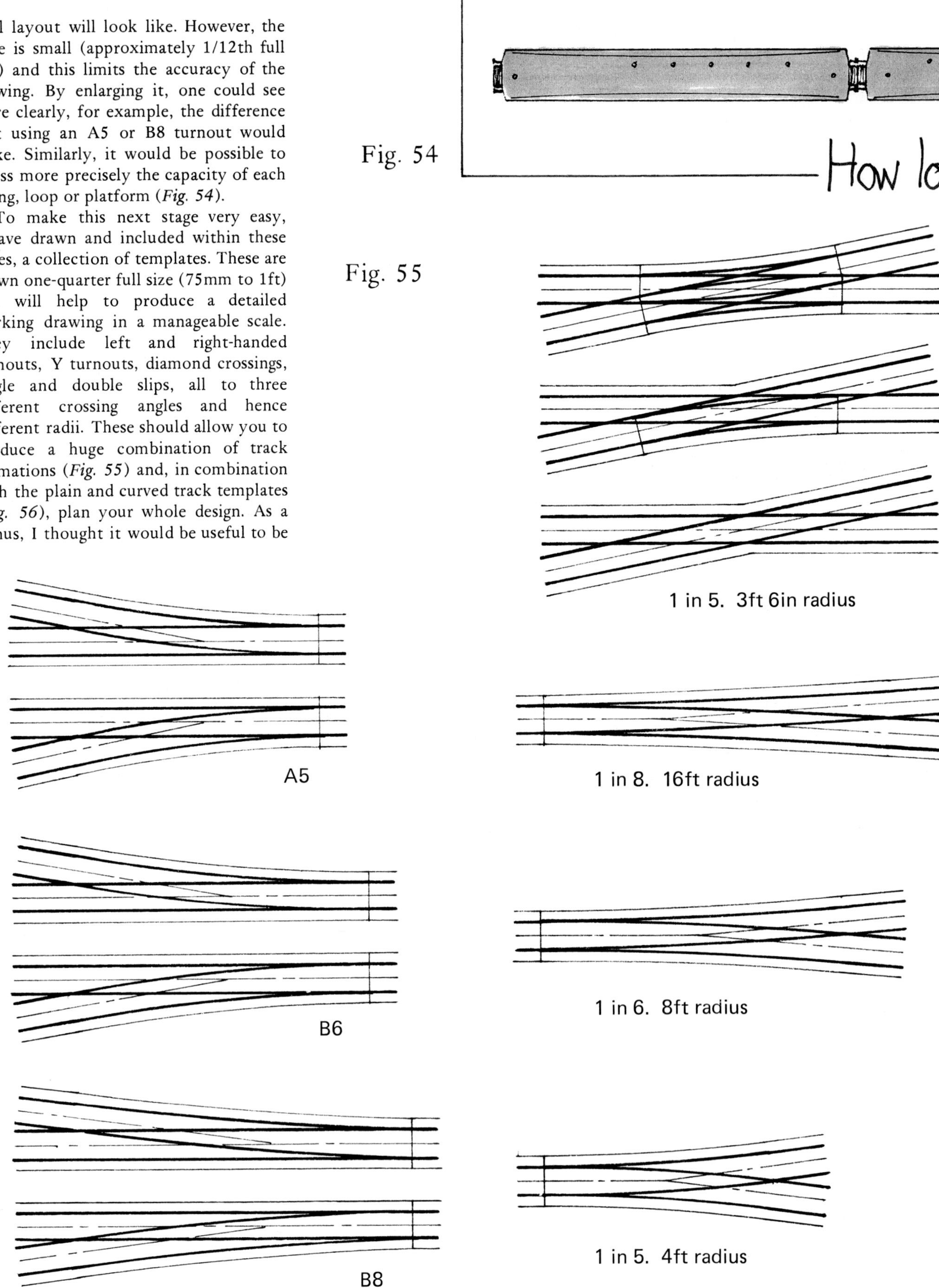

Fig. 54

Fig. 55

Radii quoted for 4mm scale only.

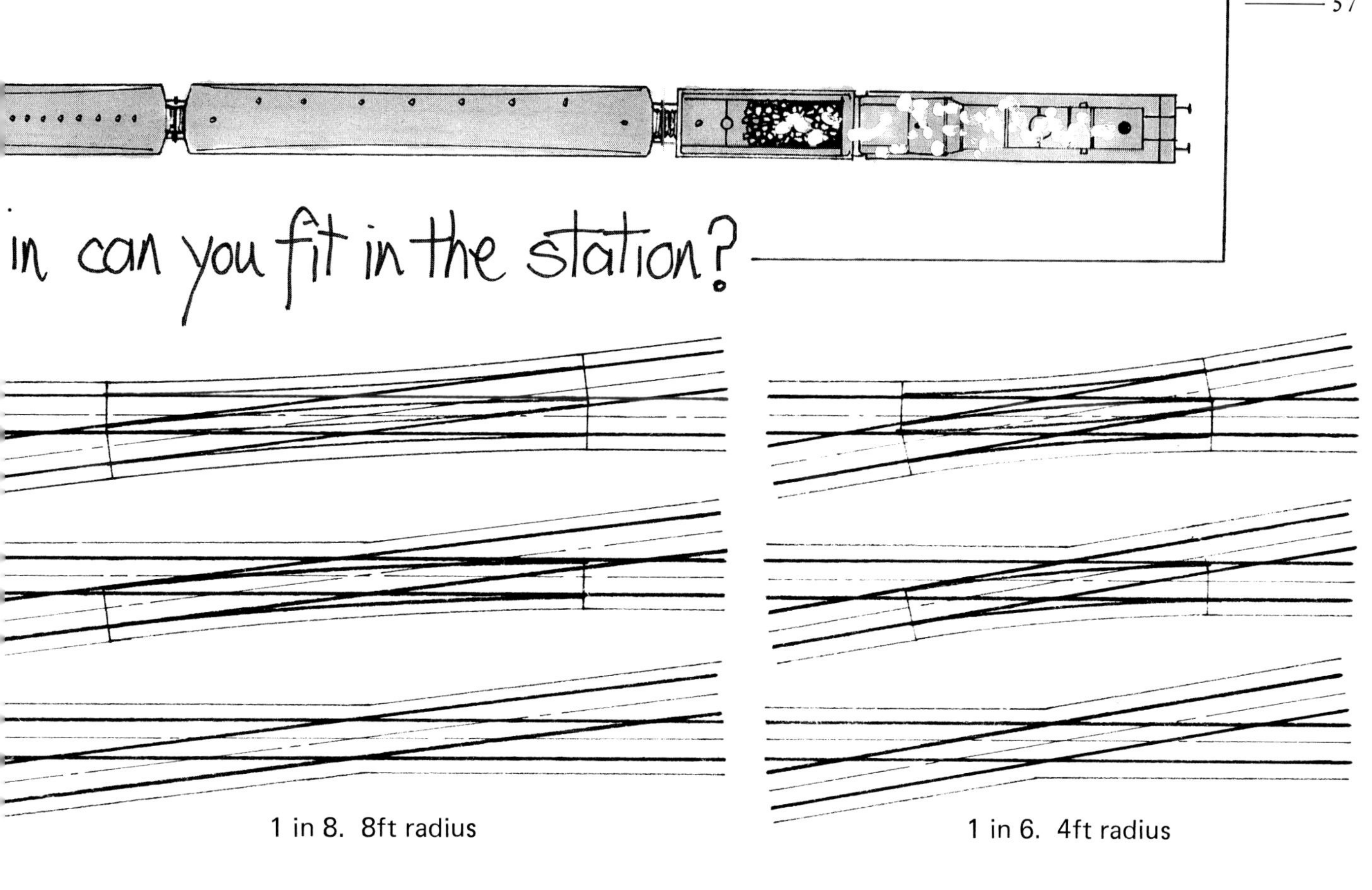
in can you fit in the station?

1 in 8. 8ft radius

1 in 6. 4ft radius

Fig. 56

16ft radius

8ft radius

4ft radius

3ft 6in radius

Radii quoted for 4mm scale only.

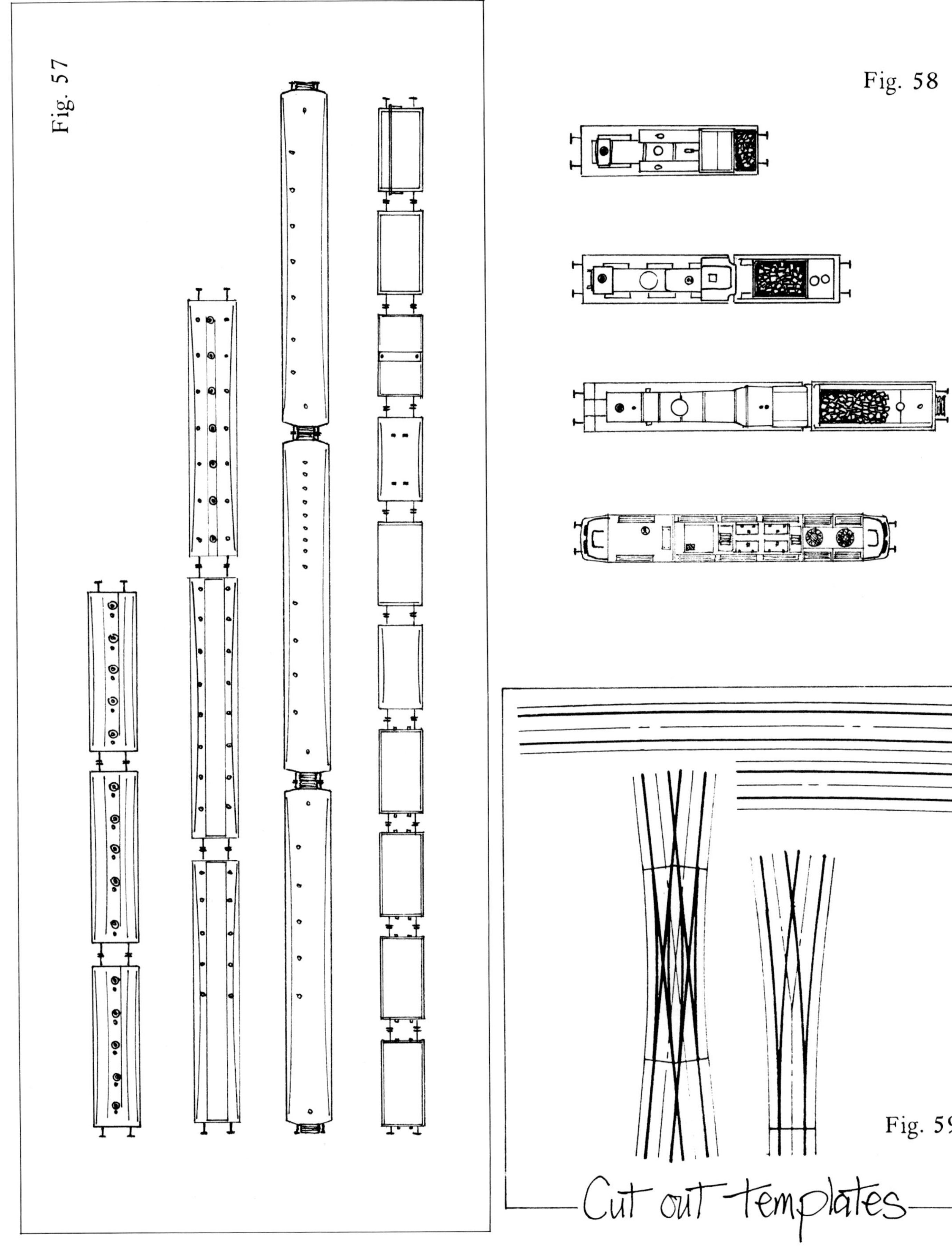

Fig. 57

Fig. 58

Fig. 59

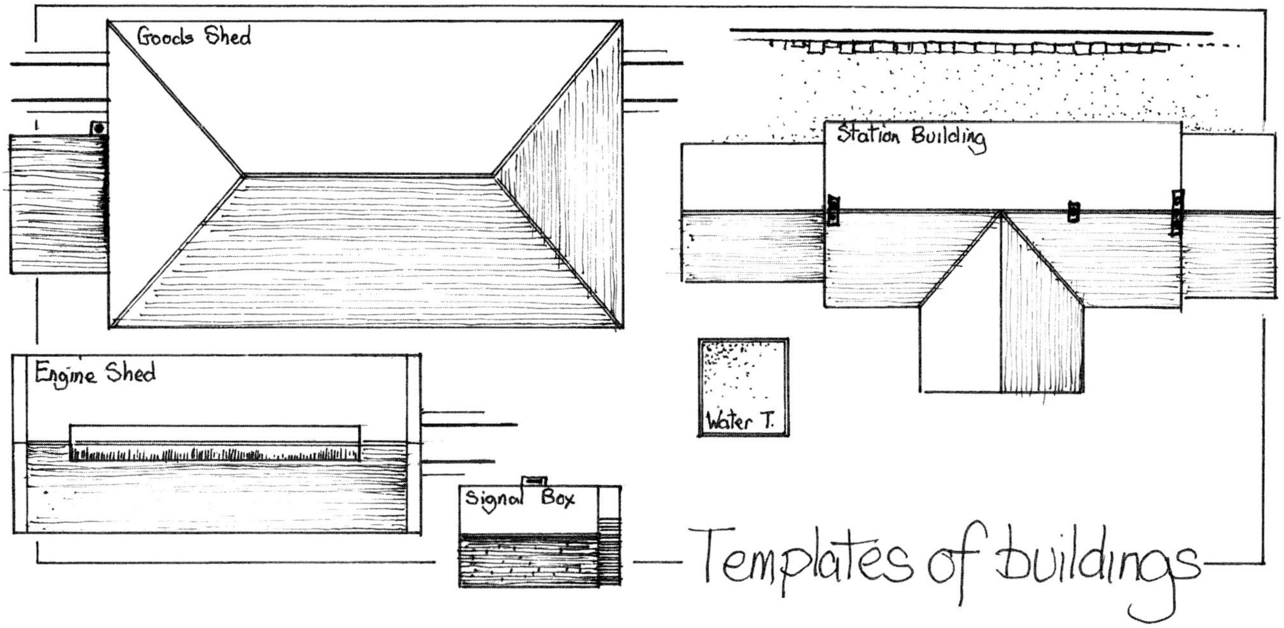

Goods Shed

Station Building

Engine Shed

Water T.

Signal Box

Templates of buildings

Fig. 60

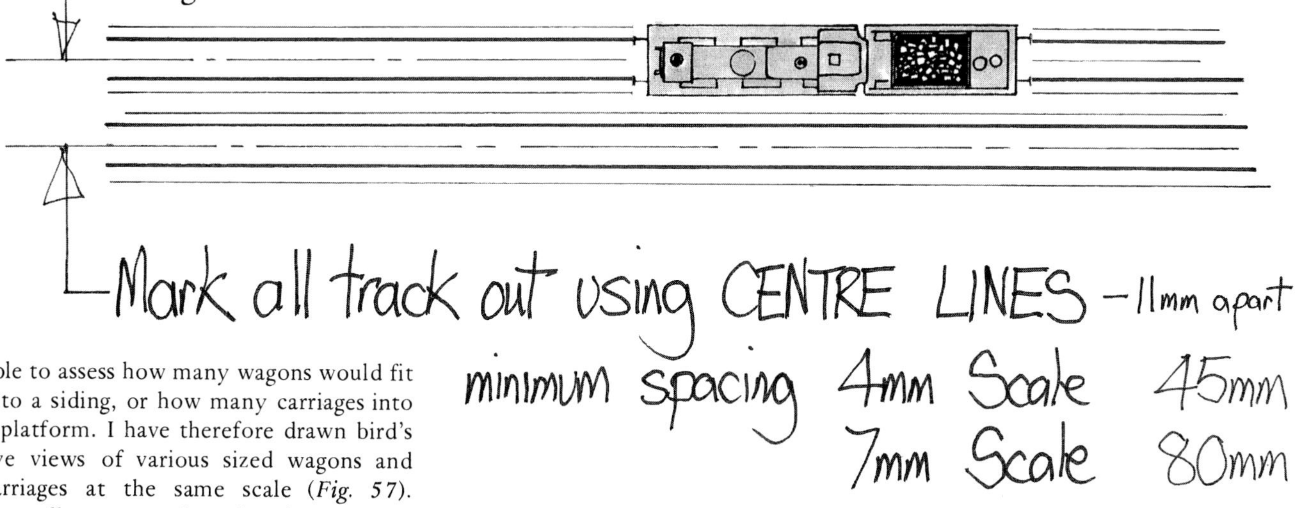

Mark all track out using CENTRE LINES – 11mm apart

minimum spacing 4mm Scale 45mm

7mm Scale 80mm

ble to assess how many wagons would fit ıto a siding, or how many carriages into platform. I have therefore drawn bird's ye views of various sized wagons and arriages at the same scale (*Fig. 57*). 'aturally, to complete the picture, plans f a tank, goods and passenger locootive, accompanied by a diesel, are cluded (*Fig. 58*).

Using these templates is simple. First hotocopy the series of templates and cut ıem out (*Fig. 59*). Take a 75mm grid ıd start drawing in the centre lines of ıe trackwork in pencil (*Fig. 60*). This ill give a rough guide to the laying of ıe turnouts as it is wise to align each entre line with its neighbour, thus radually building up the plan. Sometimes may be necessary to experiment with ifferent radius turnouts (e.g. A5 or B6)) see which fits the plan best. Note the onsiderable increase in space which is eeded in a simple crossover (*Fig. 61*). se the templates rather like we used to ay with our old Hornby tinplate track;

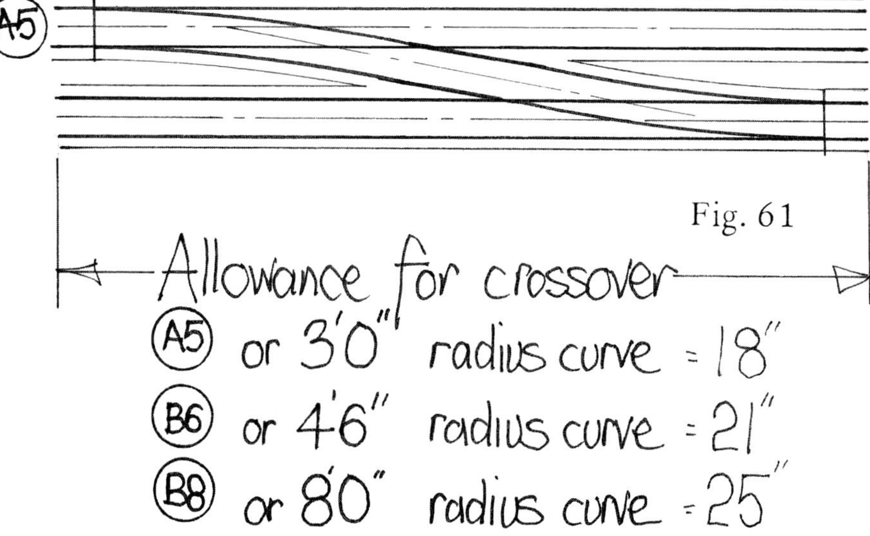

Fig. 61

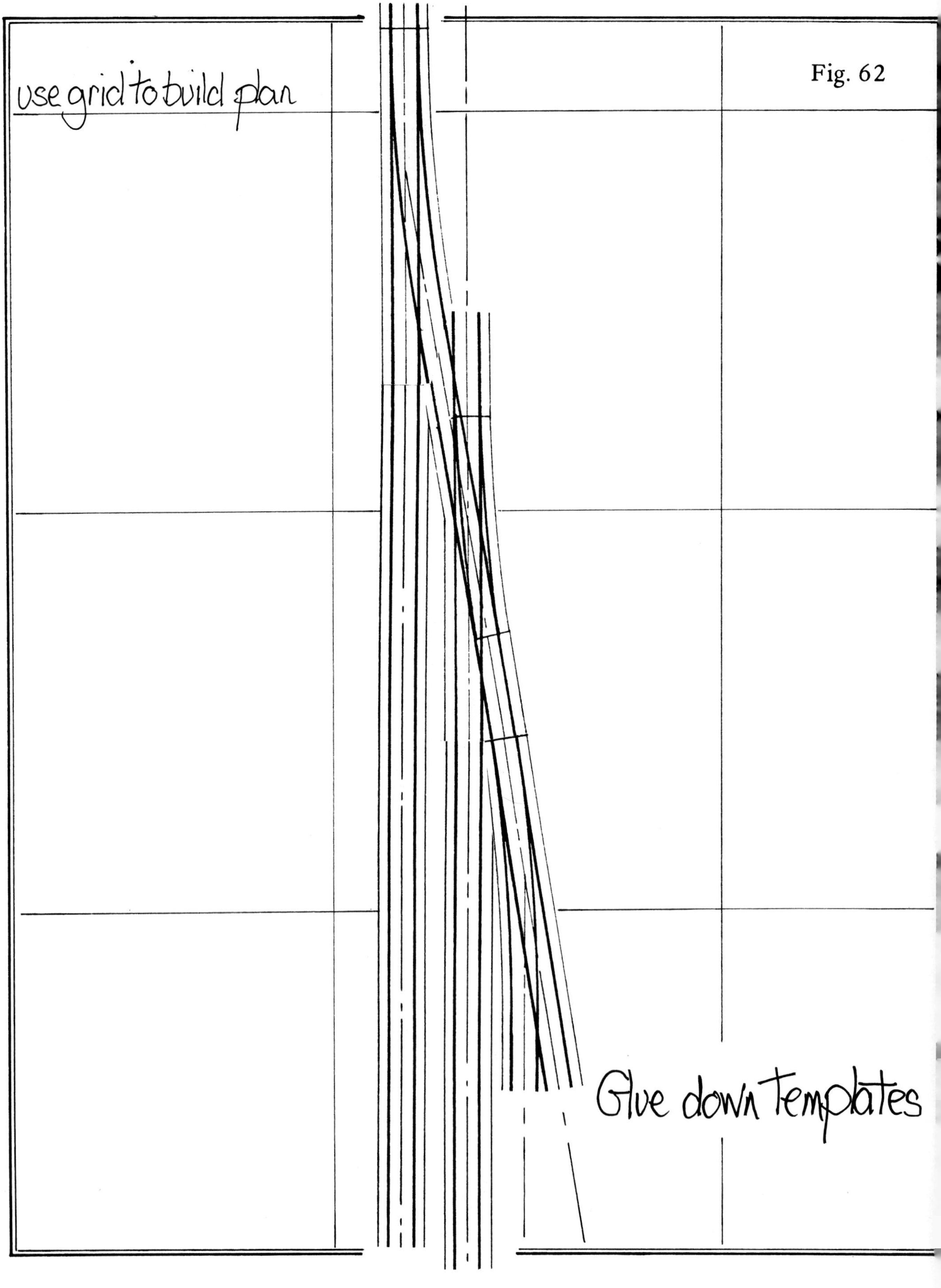

Fig. 62

use grid to build plan

Glue down Templates

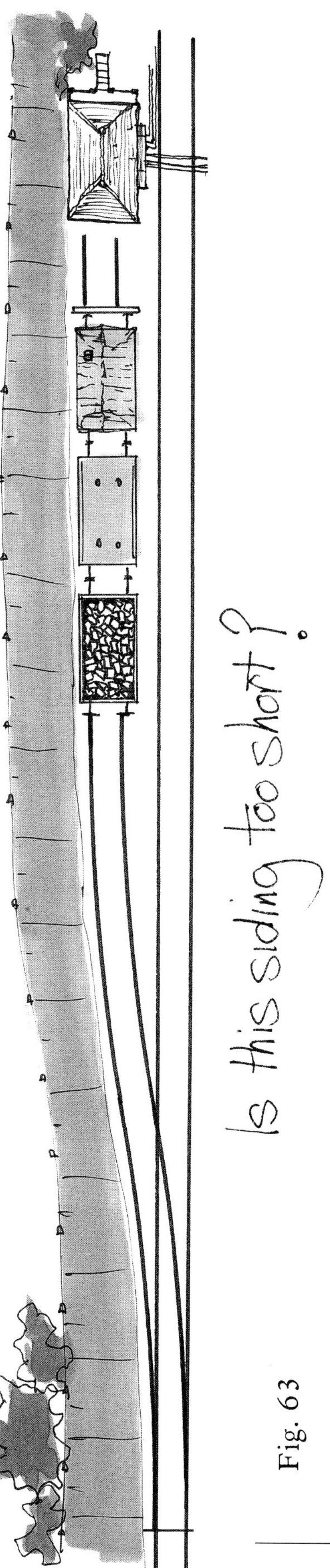
Is this siding too short?
Fig. 63

try them and experiment with them before they are finally placed in position.

Once the track formation looks about right, glue it down – a Pritt Stick is good for this (*Fig. 62*). The whole plan is progressively laid, gluing down plain track, curves, crossings, etc. until the final design has been achieved. Sometimes it may be found that it is impossible to fit the design into the space available (*Fig. 63*) and changes will have to be made. This is the very reason for working to a large and more accurate scale.

Around the trackwork, detail can be added. The platforms are an obvious next step, and working to the larger scale it is easy to work out the correct allowance to be made for them. The very narrowest of platforms were 6ft wide but these were at particularly restricted sites like halts. Twelve feet should generally be considered the minimum (*Fig. 64*). Island platforms were the same minimum dimensions, and it is also worth noting the space removed from platform length by the slopes at the ends (*Fig. 65*). If an island platform is to retain its minimum 12ft width to the end, the distance required from the toe (end) of the nearest turnout to the beginning of the platform is quite large. An A5

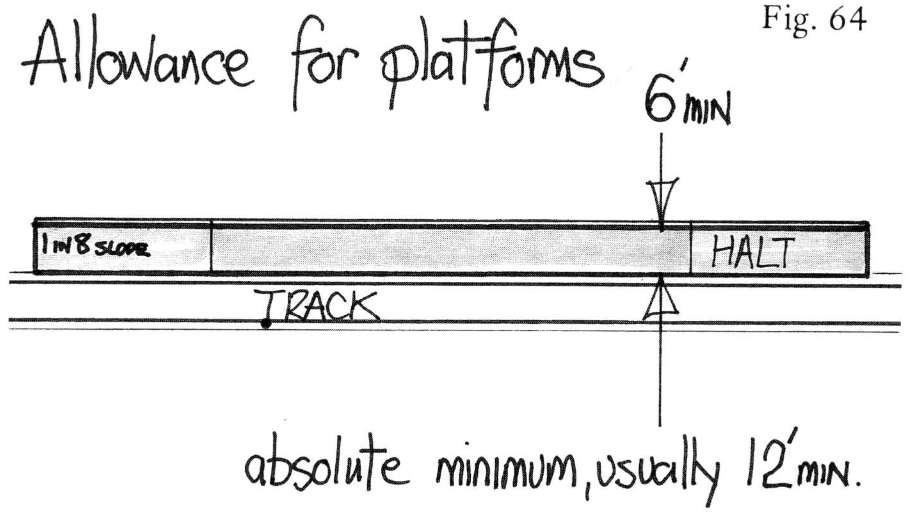

Fig. 64

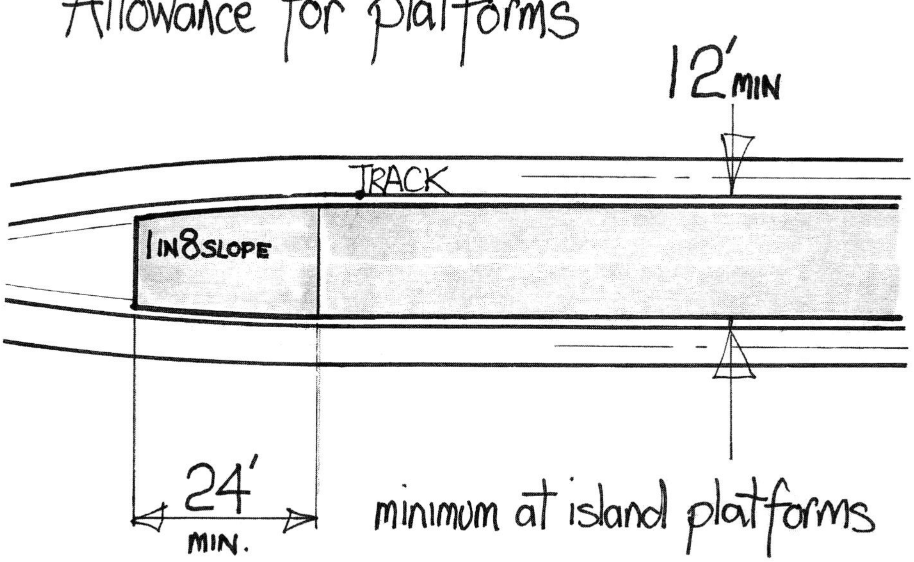

Allowance for platforms

6′ MIN

1 IN 8 SLOPE

HALT

TRACK

absolute minimum, usually 12′ MIN.

Fig. 65

Allowance for platforms

12′ MIN

TRACK

1 IN 8 SLOPE

24′ MIN.

minimum at island platforms

turnout (maintaining a 3ft radius curv would be 27 inches, whereas a lir leading from a B8 turnout would enter curve with an 8ft radius and occupy 3 inches (*Fig. 66*).

Similarly, the allowance needed avoid one train hitting another should b considered when thinking about tl number of wagons or carriages that ca be placed in a siding. In a simple situatic where a line diverges at an angle from tl turnout, a 3ft radius (A5) turnout nee a space of 12.5 inches, whereas an 8 radius (B8) turnout requires 20 inch (*Fig. 67*). These different demands c space become quite noticeable as the pla grows and the allowances are adde together. Look at what happens if siding folds back parallel to an adjace line (*Fig. 68*) or when this happens in bank of sidings such as in a goods ya (*Fig. 69*).

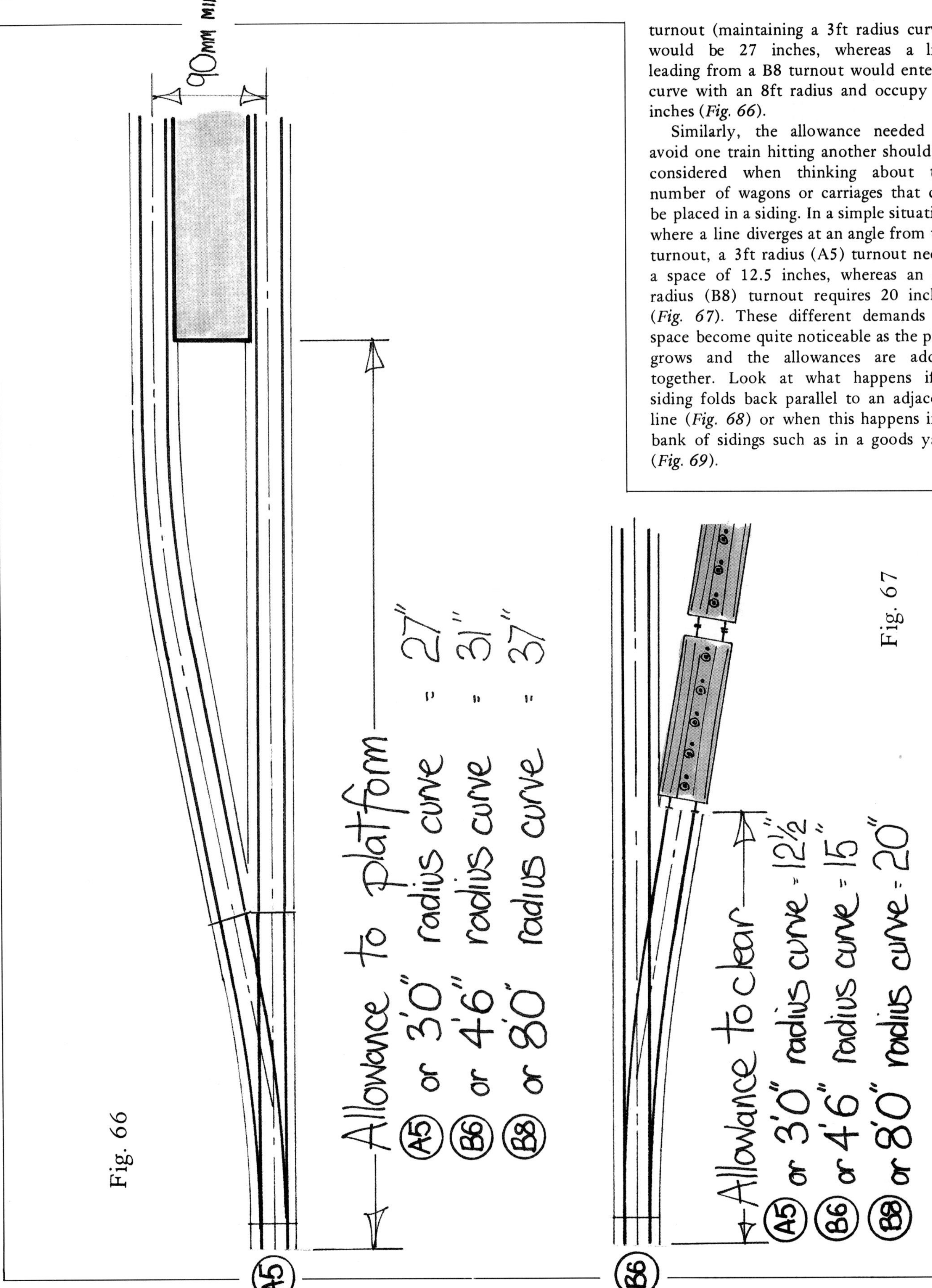

Fig. 66

Fig. 67

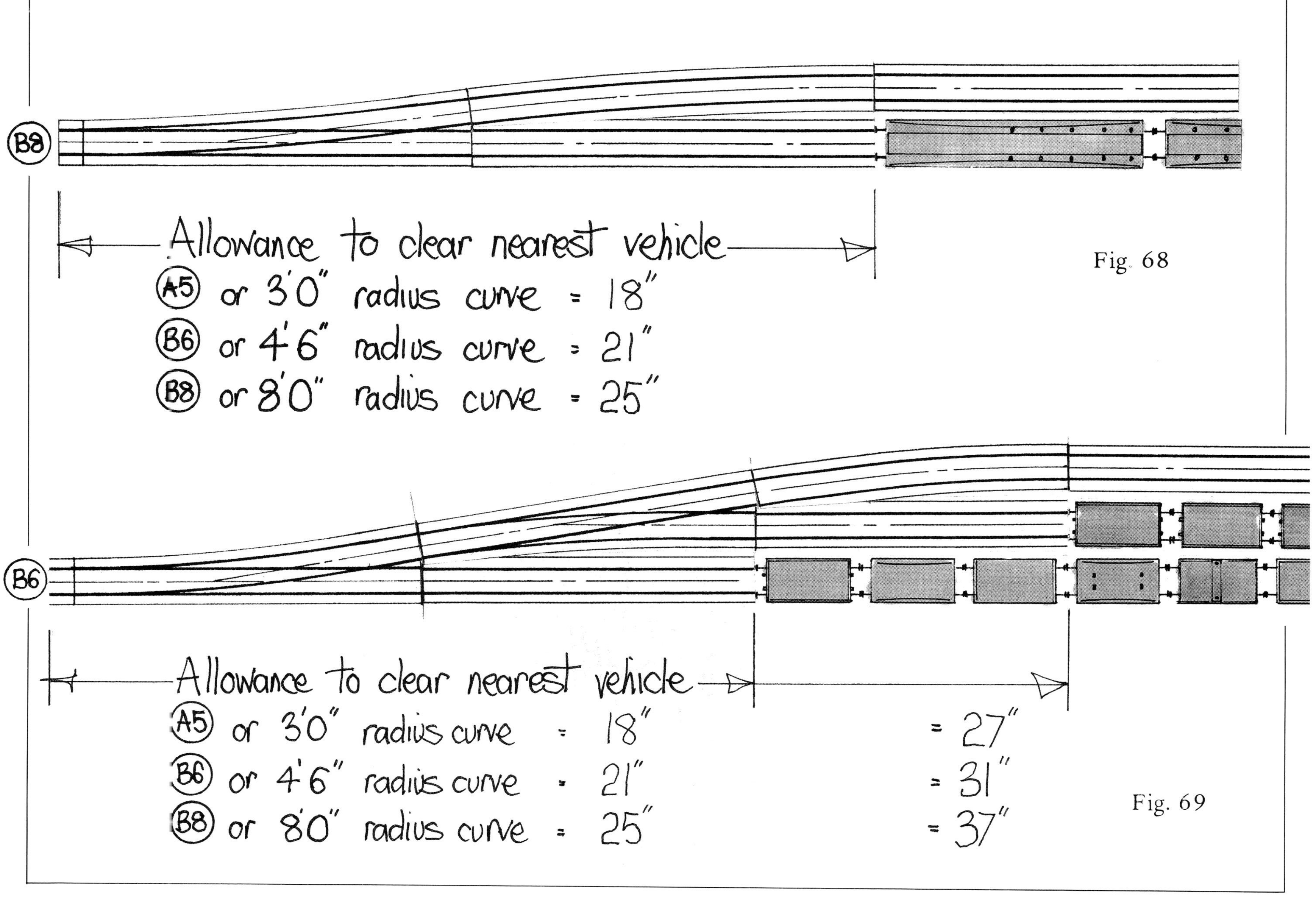
B8
Allowance to clear nearest vehicle
A5 or 3'0" radius curve = 18"
B6 or 4'6" radius curve = 21"
B8 or 8'0" radius curve = 25"
B6
Allowance to clear nearest vehicle
A5 or 3'0" radius curve = 18" = 27"
B6 or 4'6" radius curve = 21" = 31"
B8 or 8'0" radius curve = 25" = 37"

Fig. 68

Fig. 69

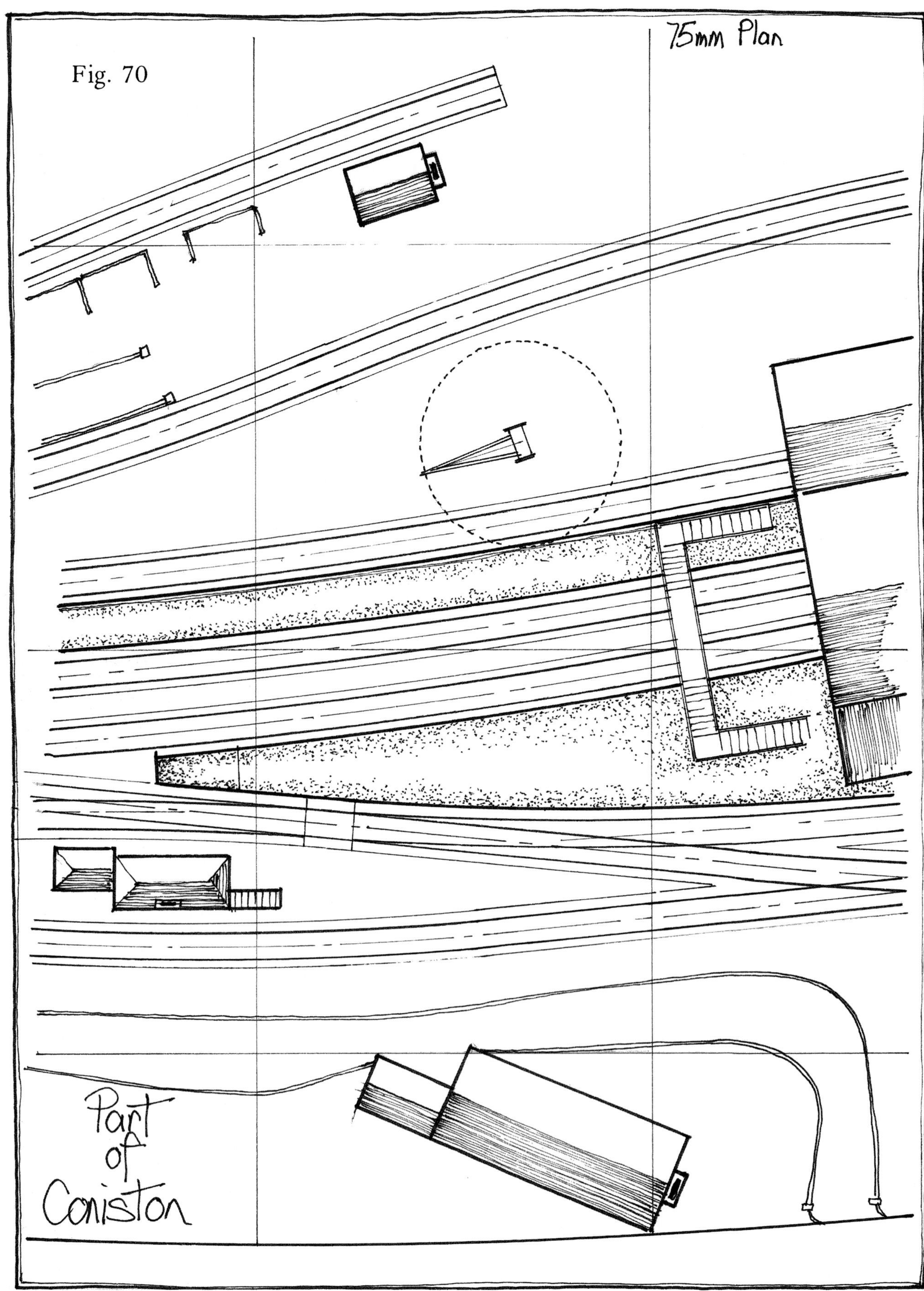
75mm Plan
Part of Coniston

Fig. 70

	2mm SCALE	4mm SCALE	7mm SCALE
25mm PLANNING GRID REPRESENTS	6" 1/6 FULL SIZE	12" 1/12 FULL SIZE	21" 1/21 FULL SIZE
75mm PLANNING GRID REPRESENTS	6" 1/2 FULL SIZE	12" 1/4 FULL SIZE	21" 1/7 FULL SIZE
TURNOUT RADIUS			
A5	1'6"	3'	5'3"
B6	2'3"	4'6"	7'10"
B8	4'	8'	14'

Fig. 71

The end result of all this planning will e a design that can realistically be turned nto a layout. Mistakes are best made now nd not once the baseboards have been uilt (*Fig. 70*).

LANS, GRIDS AND SCALES

t is perhaps important to stress the elationship between the size of the grids use and the scale of the model – this nay seem confusing. I have used two grid izes, one with 25mm squares for initial lanning and another with 75mm squares or detailed planning. In 4mm scale (OO, M, P4 gauges) both grids will always epresent 12 inches whereas in 2mm scale N gauge) it is 6 inches and in 7mm scale O gauge) 21 inches. Thus a plan which overs 10 squares would be 10ft long in mm scale, 5ft long in 2mm scale and 7ft 6in long in 7mm scale. Another way f looking at it would be that the 25mm lanning grid is one twelfth full size in mm scale whereas the 75mm grid is a quarter full size. For other scales look at the accompanying chart (*Fig. 71*).

DIVIDING THE PLAN INTO BASEBOARDS

Once I am satisfied with the track layout and have sketched in the buildings, roads and trees, I start to think about dividing the model over the various baseboards. I believe that it is important to consider boards of paired equal length as this will allow you to bolt them together face-to-face for storage or transport (*Fig. 72*). Lydham Heath was simply cut in two, leaving each board 4ft 6in x 3ft 3in. These may seem rather large, but with my method of baseboard construction, they are light and easily manageable. I mentioned in *Landscape Modelling* that

Fig. 72

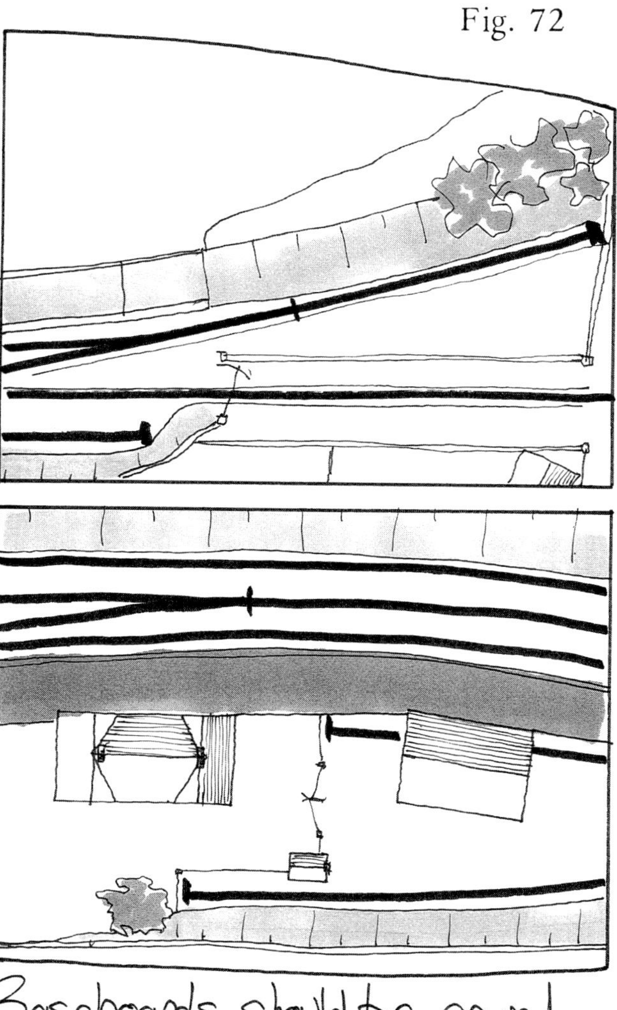

Baseboards should be equal in length

5ft x 3ft seemed an ideal maximum size if the layout is to be moved, fitting as it does lengthways in the back of a hatchback car like an Astra, or across the width of a van like a Renault Traffic or Transit (*Fig. 73*). The 3ft width *did* fit my Astra but is unfortunately a shade wide for its replacement, a Mazda 323F. So check! Whatever the size of the layout, even if it needs a van to move the whole thing, I like to think that I can at least move the individual boards by car, which should also mean that I can get them out of my railway room, down the stairs and through the back door!

The design will have to be divided into these 5ft x 3ft (or similar) units. It is important when doing this to avoid turnouts and bridges at the split point, and to look for convenient ways of disguising the joints that would arise (*Fig. 74*). You will see that I decided to split Inkerman Street by dividing the width in half and the length into three (*Fig. 75*). The length of each board was determined by the need to avoid turnouts and bridges, hence the two different sizes. I could, however, have sliced the length of the layout into six, and made each board the full width of the layout, as was the case with Petherick (*Fig. 76*),

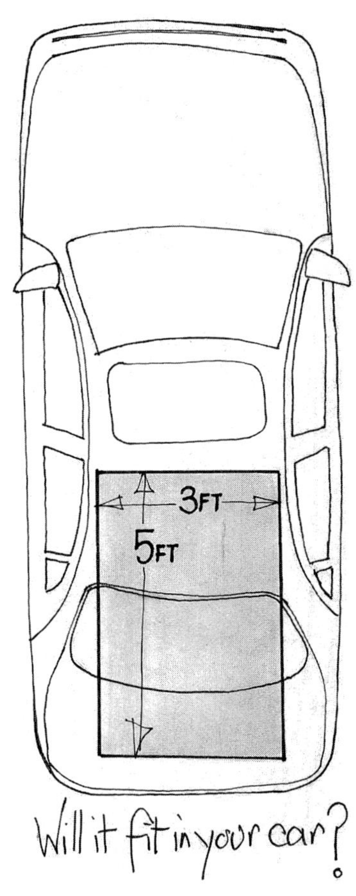

but this would have left me with rather lot of awkward baseboard joins and this i the most important thing to avoid.

MOCKING UP A DESIGN

Although I find I can visualise the fin model from a plan quite well, it is usefu to mock up the design before yo commit yourself to its construction. T do this, easily-worked materials ar important, as I would not wish to wast too much time. I like to use card an expanded polystyrene to build up lan and buildings around the quarter-scal track plan to get a better feel of what th layout will finally look like. Certainly thi is a very useful exercise, for at times on can too easily assume that a hillsid would look steeper than it actually doe or the height of a building lower than i actually the case.

From this, I always go on to draw full-size plan. I remember that when w planned 'Inkerman Street', Paul Kara and I crawled around for some time o the floor with lengths of wallpaper and piece of 2in by 1in timber (using it as trackbed gauge), gradually drawing ou the plan. We checked the length c turnouts in particular, as it is too easy t draw them in a rather compressed manne

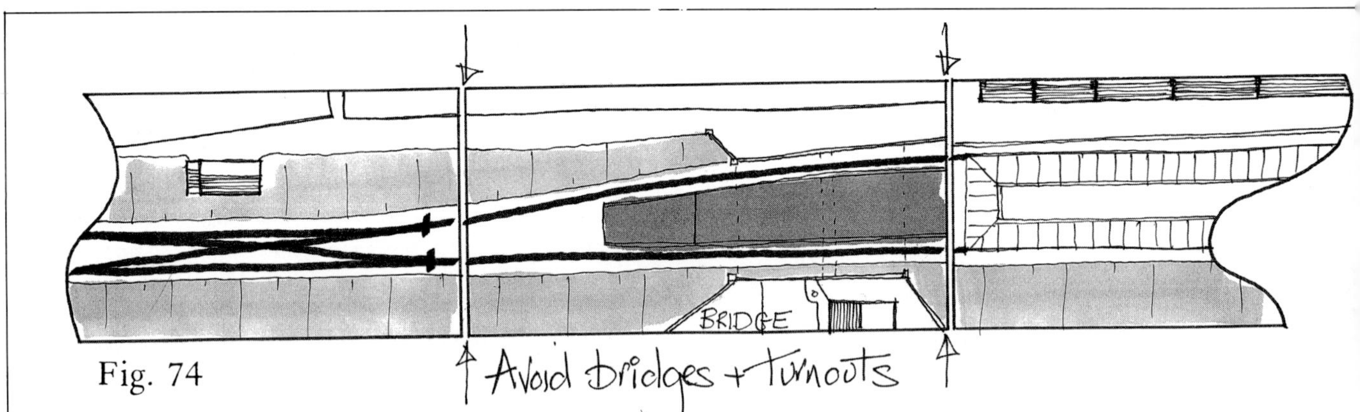

BRIDGE

Fig. 74

Avoid bridges + turnouts

INKERMAN ST.
7mm Scale

BASEBOARD JOINTS : Divide the width in half

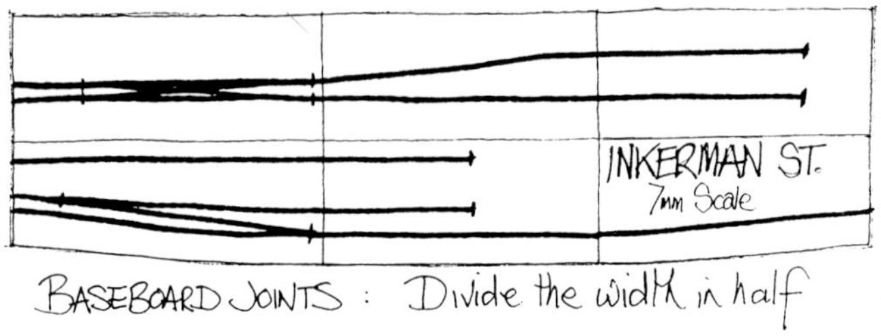

Fig. 75

Fig. 76

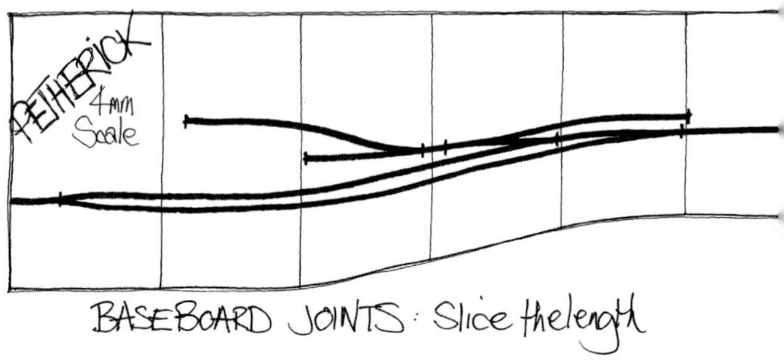

PETHERICK
4mm Scale

BASEBOARD JOINTS : Slice the length

mistake that would have unfortunate esults when the track was laid.

We did one more piece of mocking-up vhen building 'Inkerman Street' which ould be a useful exercise when building ny layout. We made full-size replicas of he buildings in white card – and they ooked good. They were simple, just cut rom 1.5mm thick card with a metal rule nd scalpel. The sides were laid out in one ong strip, folded at the corners and oined with a tab (*Fig.* 77). These were nocked out very quickly (about 15 mins building) but they gave us a great nsight into what the layout would look ke. This was quite a dramatic exercise nd brought home to us the sheer size of 'mm scale.

After all this thought and care, you an now step successfully and confidently owards building the layout.

Fig. 77

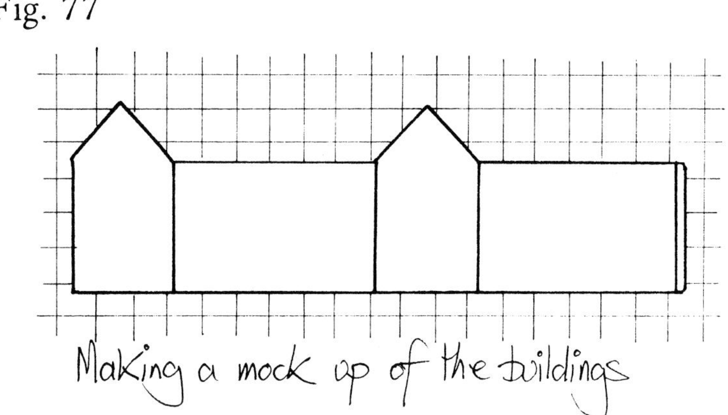
Making a mock up of the buildings

A mock-up of the interchange between the narrow gauge and standard gauge at Blaenau Ffestiniog takes shape.

A completed mock-up of my Mytholme design (page 73) which was intended as a small 7mm scale layout. This model has enabled me to picture the completed layout and form a reasoned opinion about the design.

PART TWO

Developing a Layout Design

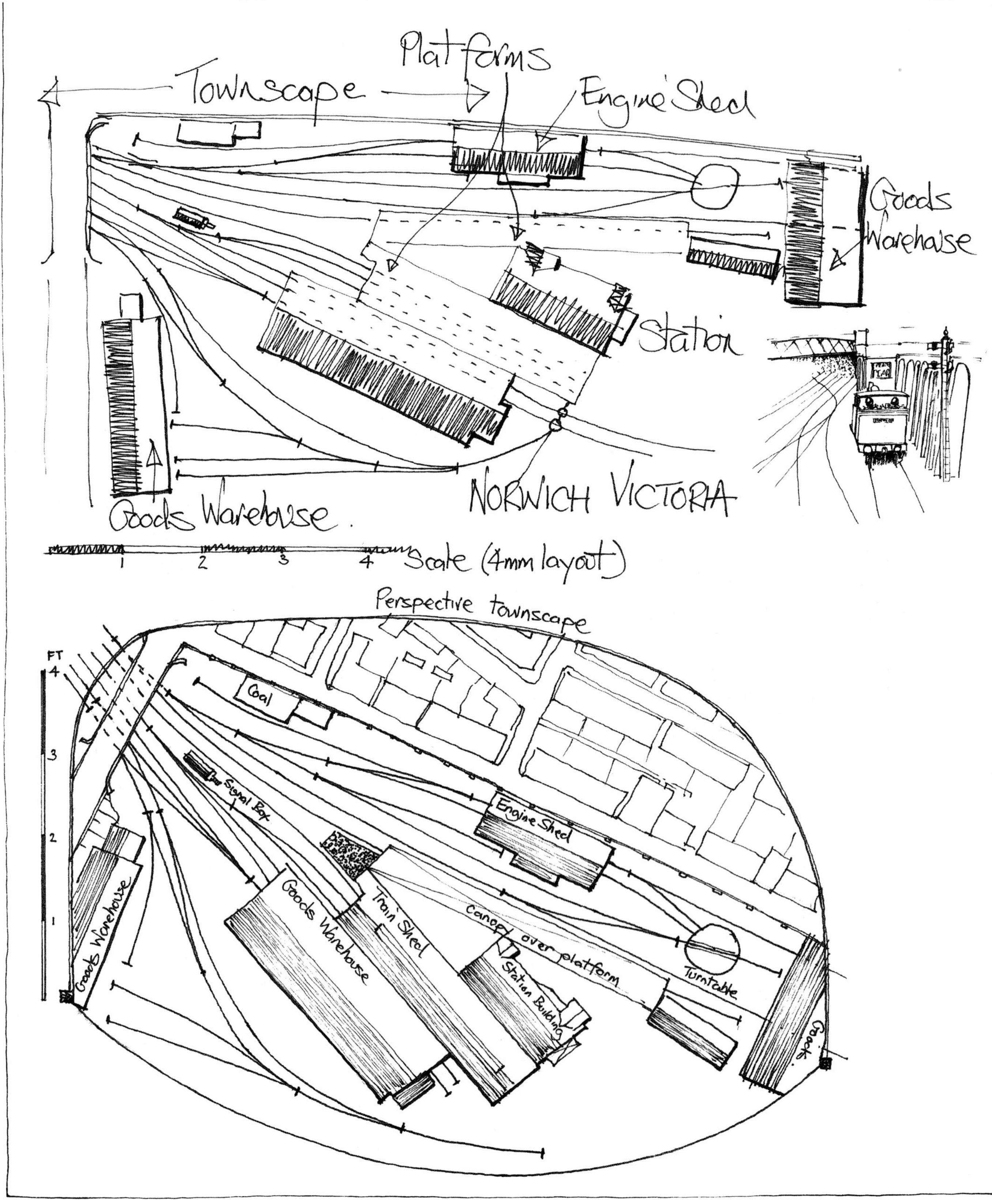

MIDHURST

Midhurst was an interesting and quite unusual station (built by the London & South Western Railway) not least because the line extended beyond the platforms to provide a connection with the neighbouring London Brighton & South Coast Railway station. This would give scope for some interesting operation, particularly in the pre-Grouping era when the different-liveried stock of each company could be seen side by side. The siding that led off to a sand pit gives further operating interest.

This prototype is in many ways ideal, the high land at the back making a good backdrop as it falls towards the front, leaving much of the station on an embankment. The buildings are attractive and the operation interesting, making Midhurst a delightful layout.

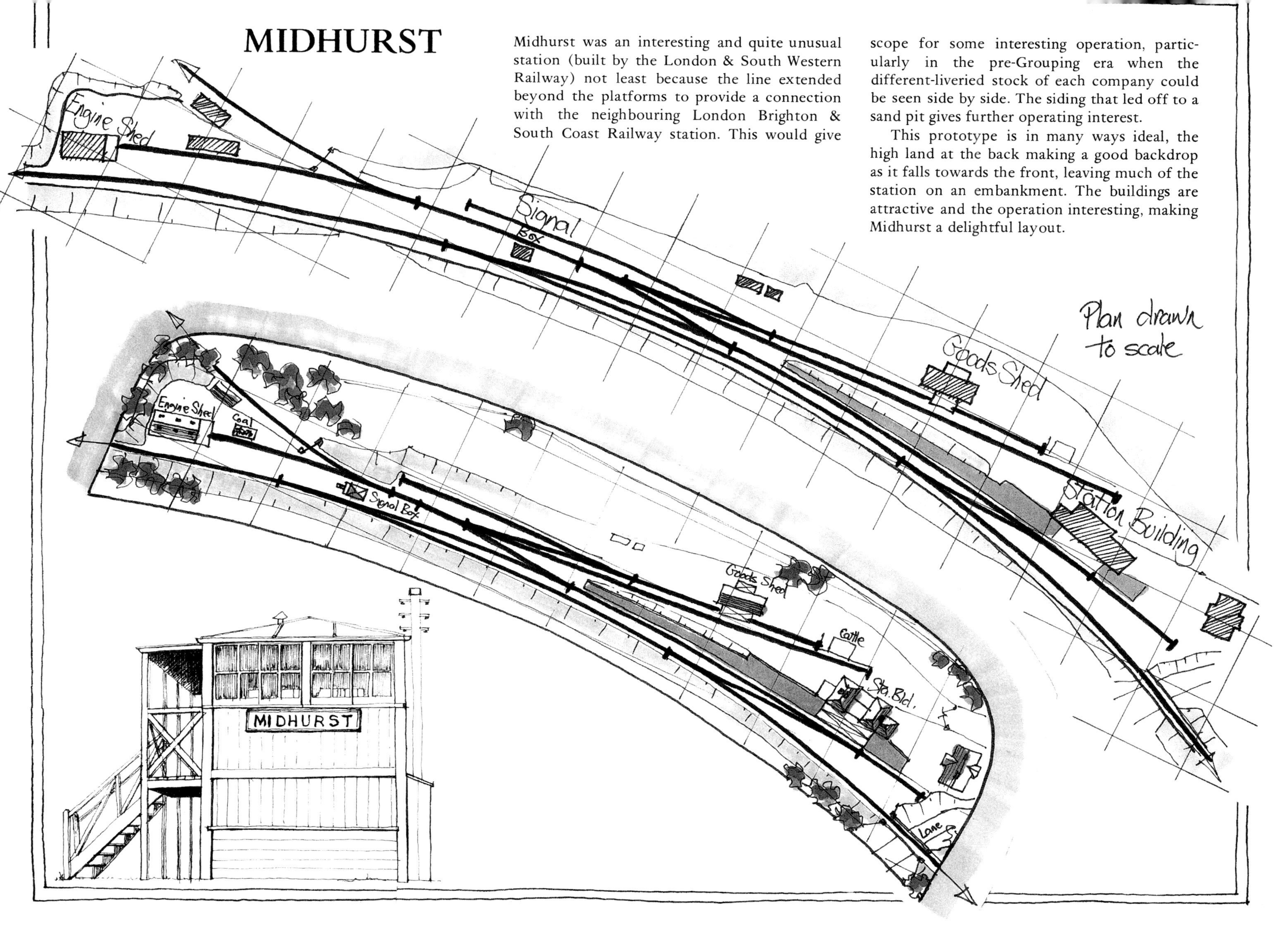

CHINLEY

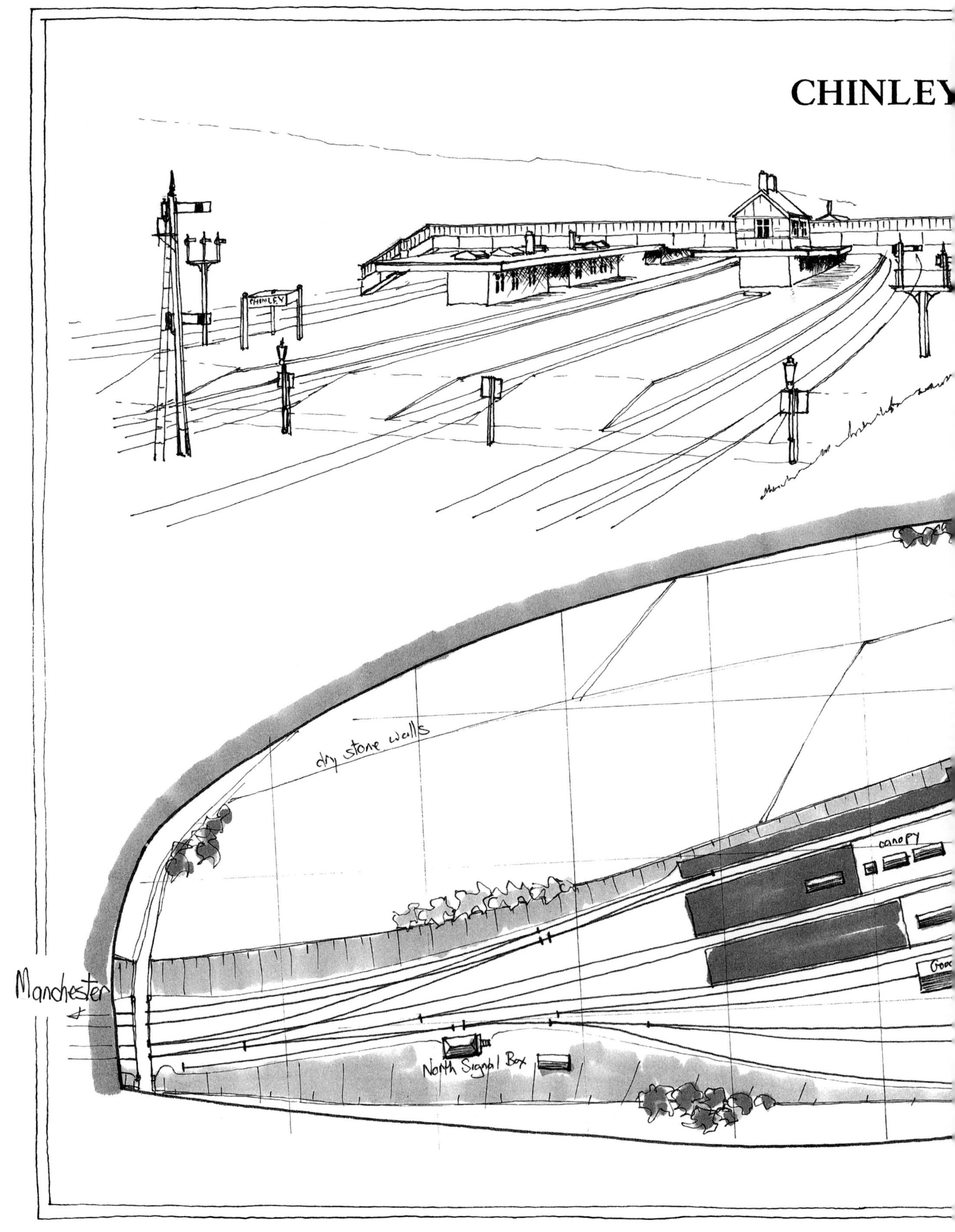
CHINLEY
dry stone walls
canopy
Manchester
North Signal Box

Situated between the junction of lines to Sheffield, Manchester, Derby and London, Chinley was a busy place. The original double-tracked line was quadrupled about the turn of the century to cope with the high increase in (particularly) passenger traffic, and with it a new station was built. Chinley was not a very populous area but the size of the station reflected its location as a convenient place to stop and change trains. Carriages were detached from London expresses and added to trains continuing their journey to Manchester and beyond. Most passenger trains stopped here, and consequently refreshment rooms were well used. Locomotives were also turned on a newly installed turntable, and watered from cranes by the platforms.

There was also plenty of goods working, mainly through mineral trains, and an engineers yard. The area was also rich in quarries which fed the railway, as did the expanding town with its growing number of businesses.

As a model this would be an exciting layout to operate, considering the fact that it is really very small. It is also scenically attractive, with the distant rain-soaked hills rolling down to the colourful canopied platforms. It strikes me as an ideal layout to model in 2mm scale, although by no means impossible in a larger scale.

I would certainly like to see the station buildings and platform canopies modelled and would enjoy watching Midland Railway engines tearing past a convincing representation of the dark, damp, sandstone retaining walls and lineside buildings. This is a diorama — a landscape and railway really worth building.

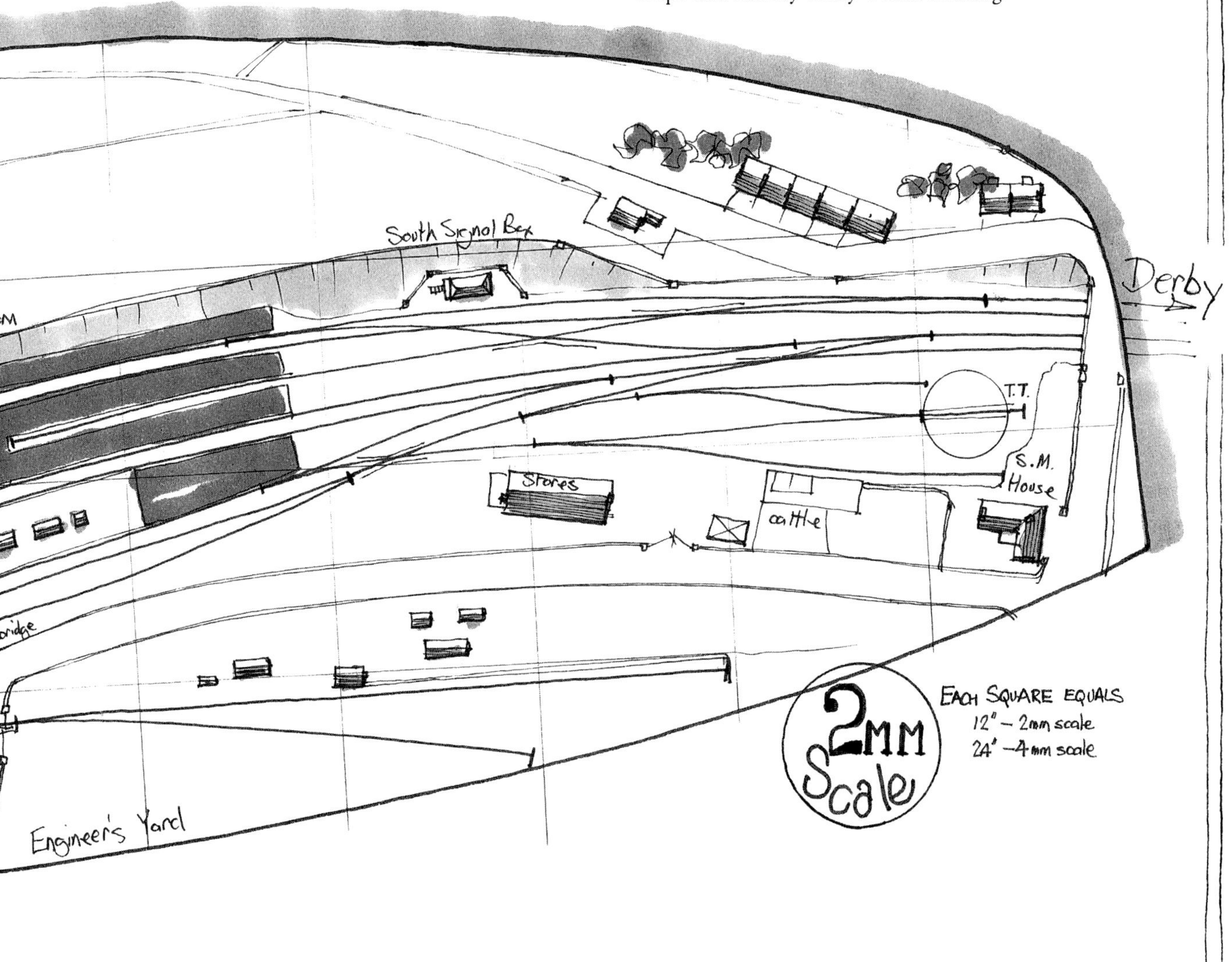

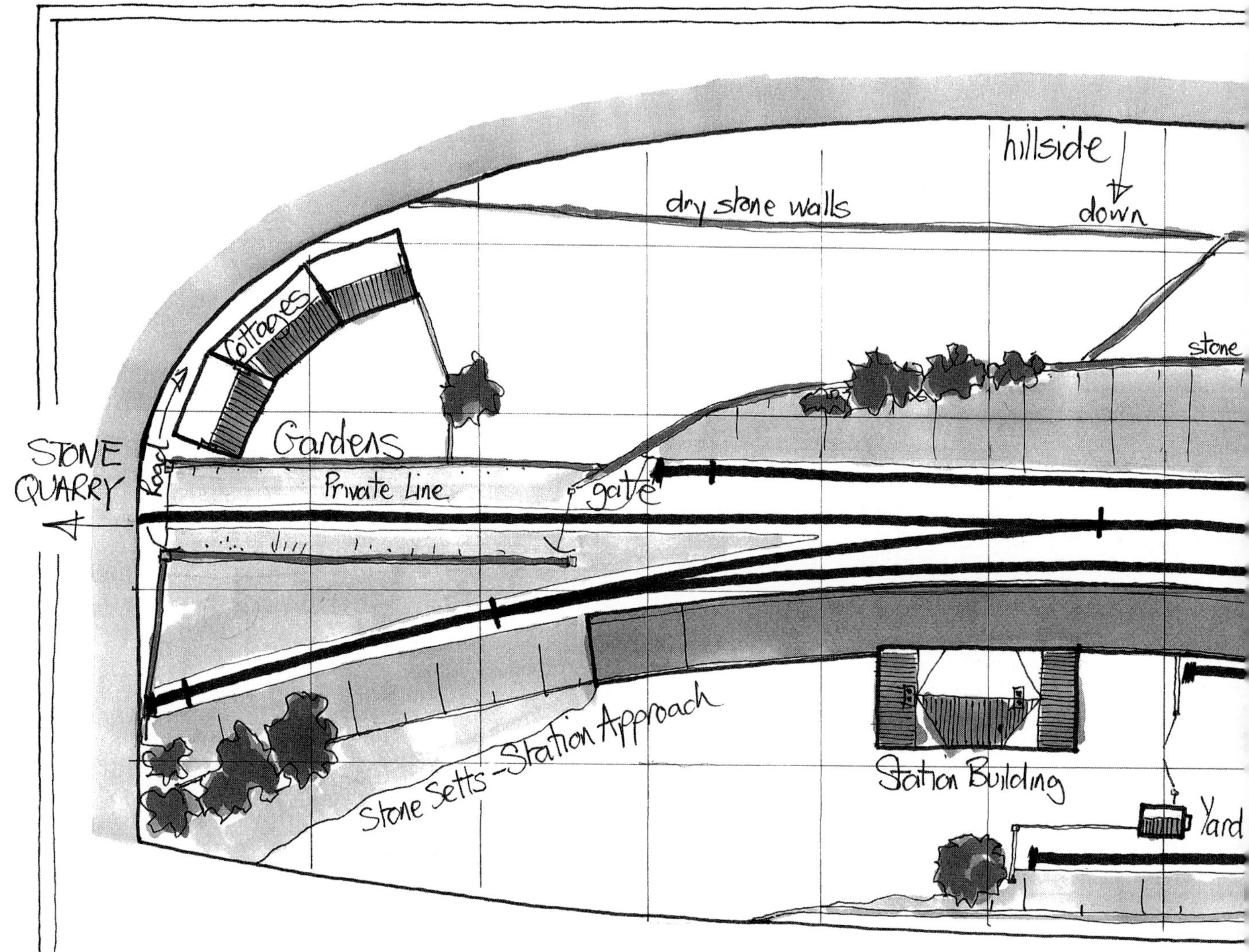

MYTHOLME

This choice easily overcomes any problems concerning availability of information about the railway — a trip with a tape measure and camera to the preserved Keighley & Worth Valley Railway would be all that is needed. However, difficulties arise when choosing a suitable location to model. I was looking for a small, characterful station with plenty of operating interest for a 7mm scale layout, but none seemed to fit the bill. So I took Oxenhope and added to it a line to a stone quarry (which I thought would bring in extra traffic), and provided another siding which would be useful for holding stone wagons or spare carriages. I borrowed the road bridge from Haworth and used the railway 'workers' cottages from Oakworth, tying them all together with a thread of dry stone walls.

As this is a small layout (only 12ft long), I thought it important to make it wide so that the hillside behind the station would create depth and allow me to model the glorious stand of trees that border the trackside. These are a spectacular sight in autumn, and this for me would be the time when I would model Mytholme (a village that didn't have a station). Despite its cramped size, I feel my design could pass as a convincing stop on this delightful branch line. I rather like this approach, and would categorise it as the modelling of a typical, rather than one particular station, by mixing elements from neighbouring stations.

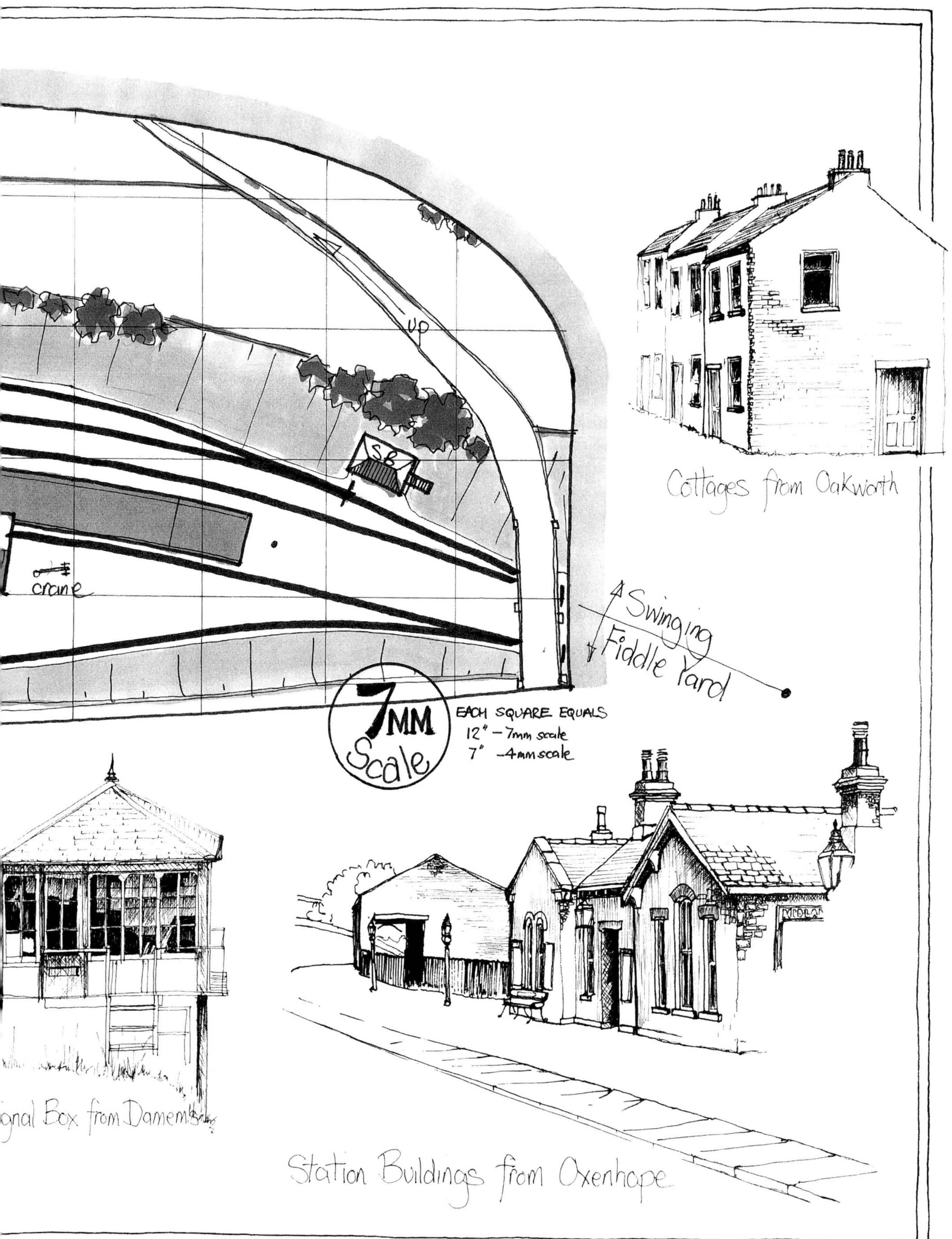

Cottages from Oakworth

gnal Box from Damems

Station Buildings from Oxenhope

CAMELOT

Camelot is clearly St. Ives, its seaside location fully exposed. It would make an ideal model on its own, but is enriched here by its role as a terminus for trains from Tresco. I like the idea of sending trains on their journey to different destinations, and this design offers the possibility of a very interesting, timetabled service. Tresco (the junction station) has much in common with Bodmin. This highly unlikely Southern line may bring back memories of trainspotting at Wadebridge but is a model-maker's fantasy. However, it is all good fun and I could imagine sitting down at the layout with a few friends, drinking mugs of tea and having a jolly good time – and why not?

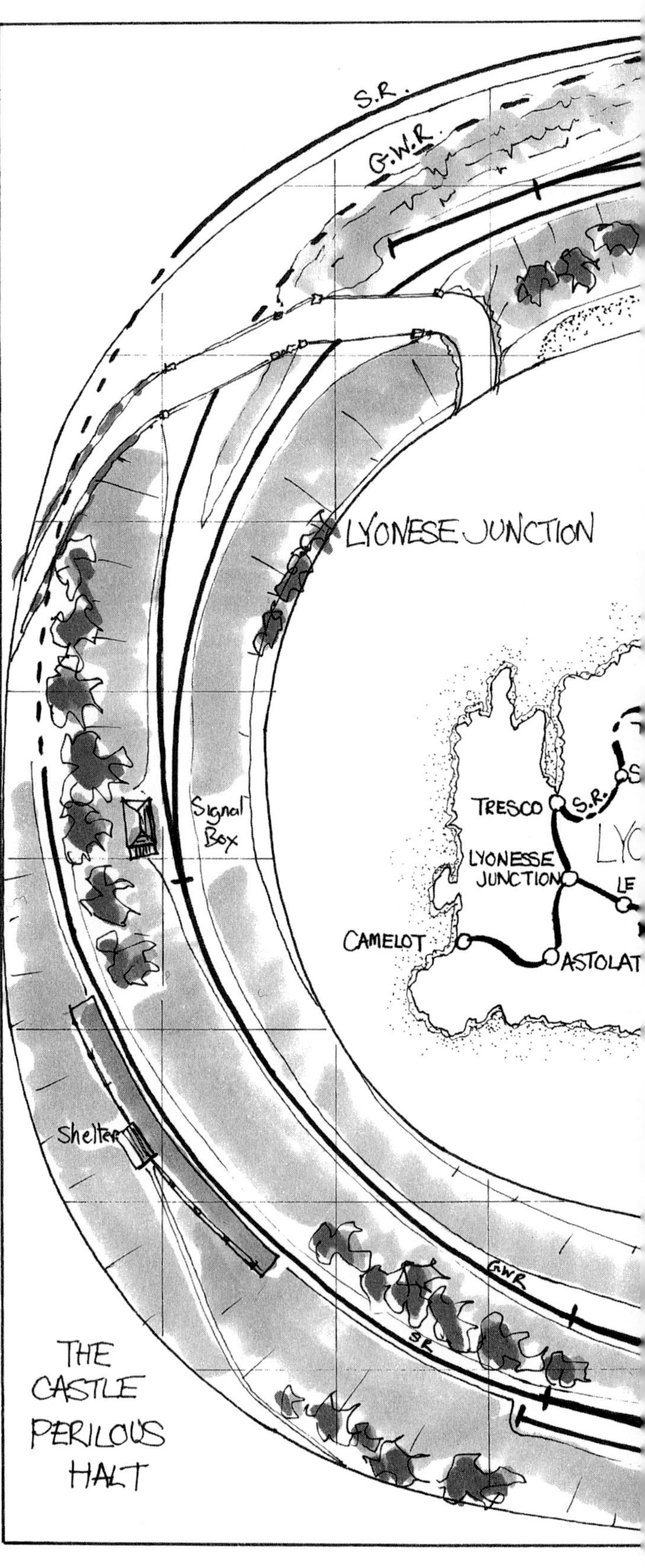

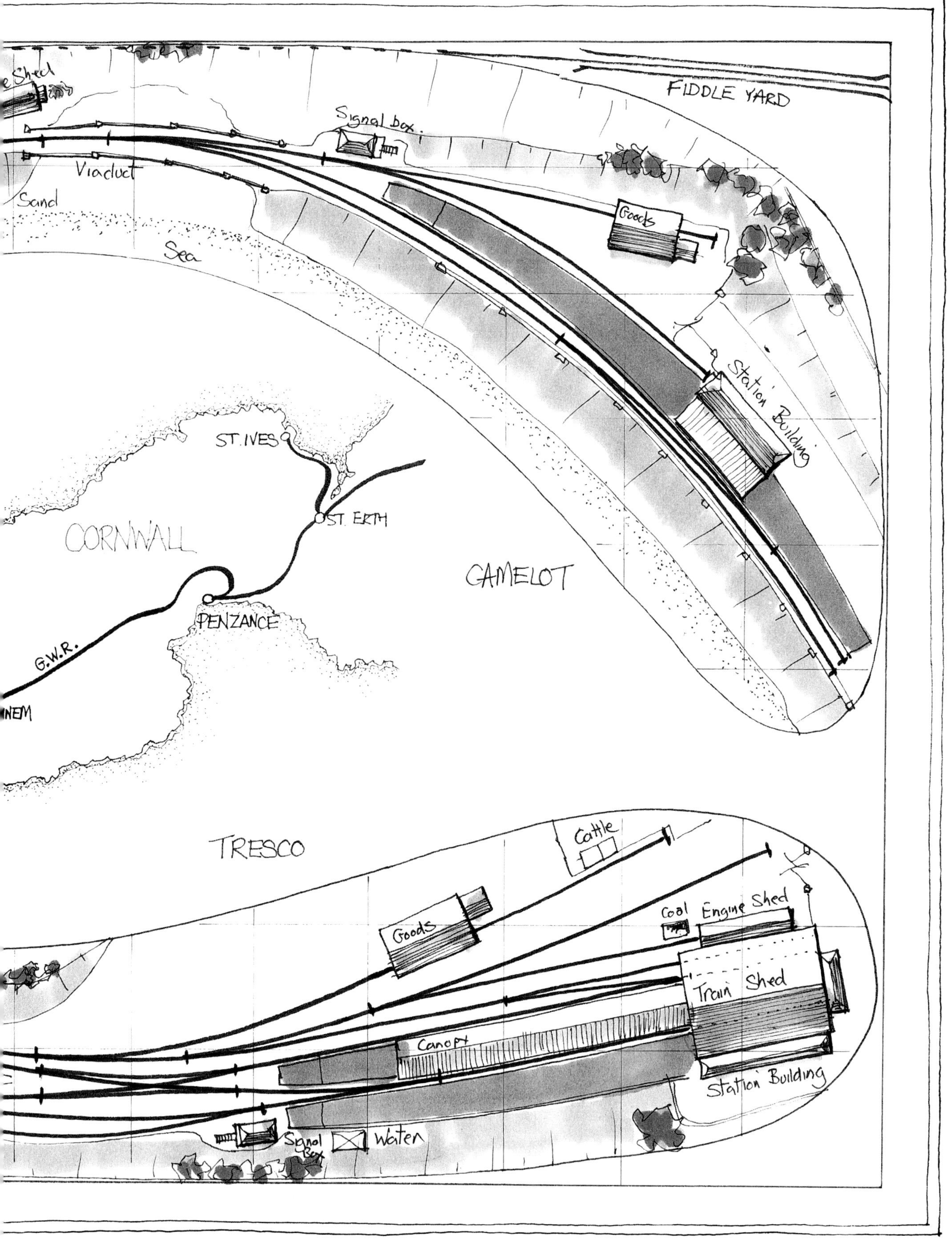
Shed
Signal box.
FIDDLE YARD
Viaduct
Sand
Goods
Sea
Station Building
ST. IVES
ST. ERTH
CORNWALL
CAMELOT
PENZANCE
G.W.R.
TRESCO
Cattle
Goods
Coal
Engine Shed
Train Shed
Canopy
Station Building
Signal Box
Water

BISHOP'S CASTLE

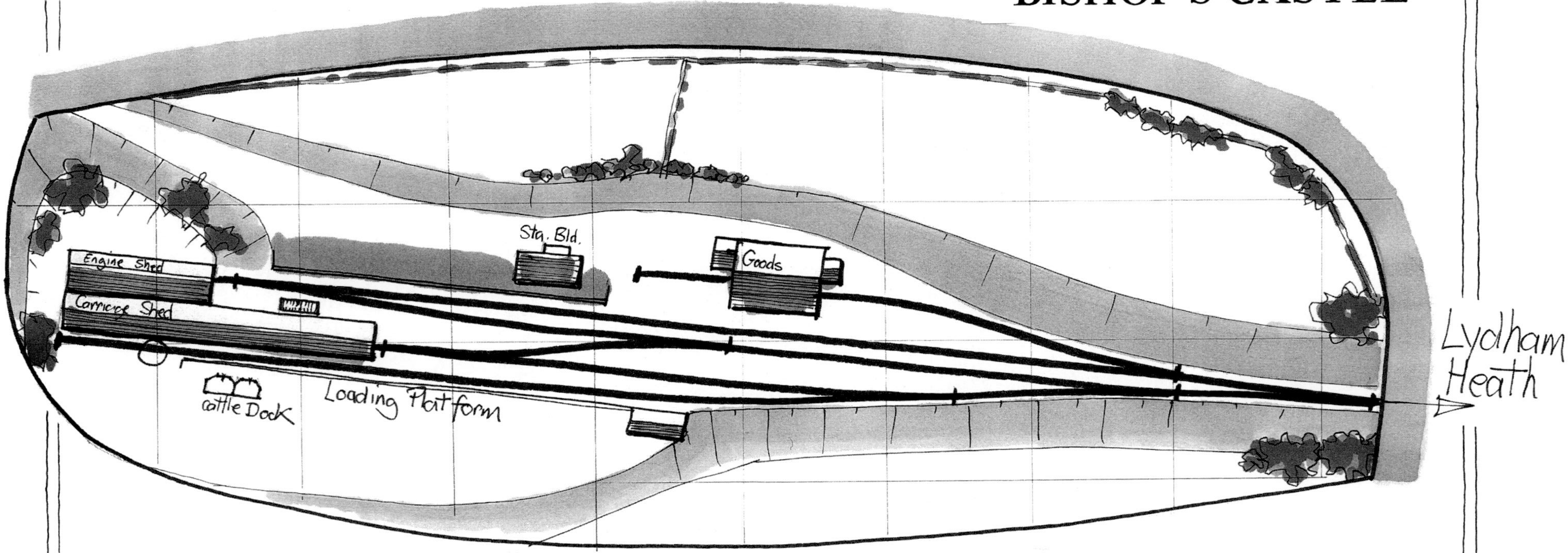

Without doubt the most appealing part of this station is the combined carriage and engine shed. This dilapidated, worn-out timber-boarded building with its corrugated iron roof is ultimately characteristic of a light railway and particularly one like the Bishop's Castle Railway. This one tatty building tells us all about the fortunes of the BCR and would have to be at the heart of any model of the station.

The site was long and narrow, ending quite conveniently in a road overbridge. However, a scale model would be large and in many ways appear rather empty. To make it more interesting I have focused on the engine-cum-carriage shed, station building and goods shed, as well as the more unusual trackwork, and reduced as much as possible the length of the model. I feel that the essential ingredients of Bishop's Castle are still present whilst the unique buildings have been emphasised in making the layout a more manageable size. Unfortunately, the road bridge had to be left out, but its role of scenic break has fallen to a clump of trees in the foreground of the layout.

ALNWICK

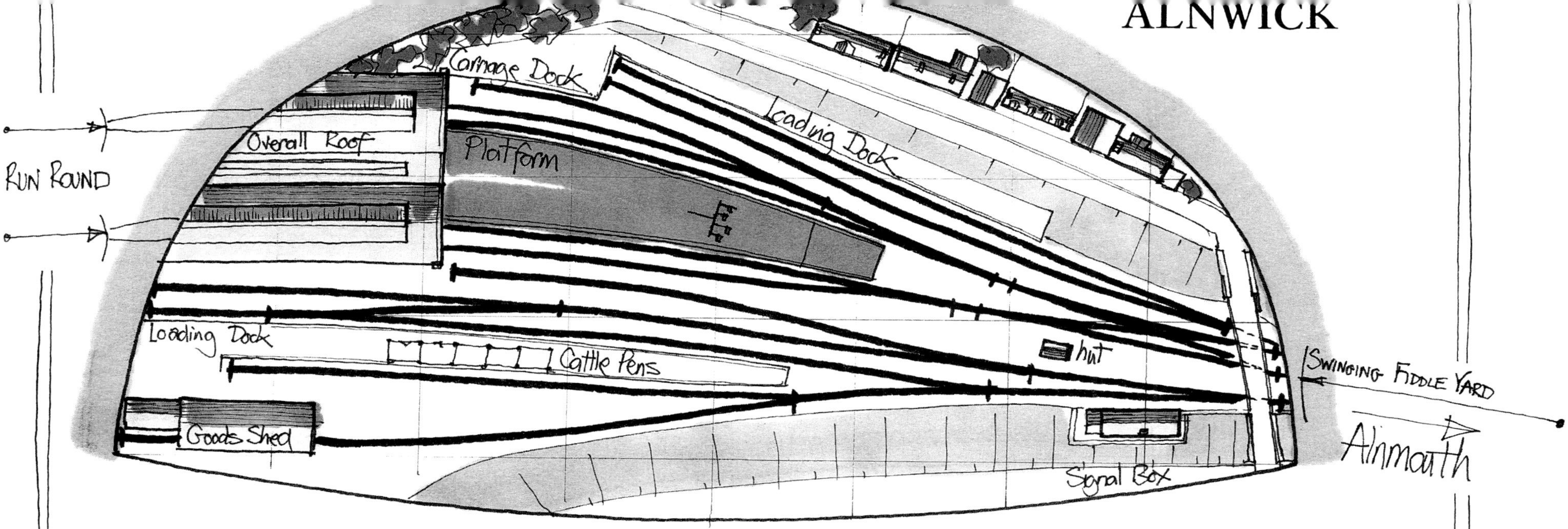

This was a rather large Northumbrian station, but by the use of fiddle yards that swing from track to track to replace turnouts, its size has been reduced to a surprisingly small 8ft. Little is lost from the operating potential of the layout: the main fiddle yard controls all shunting manoeuvres in and out of the goods yard and enables passenger trains to enter different platforms. At the other end of the model, the train shed worried me, partly because of the difficulty of uncoupling trains within it and partly because of the space it would take up. I thought about ways it could be coupled into the backscene and help to create a realistic backdrop. The idea proposed here may be unusual, but it does overcome all these problems and helps to shorten the model quite a bit.

This need to cut down size provoked a thoughtful look at the trackplan. It was clear that several sidings could be removed from the goods yard, but this was done carefully so that those that remained were of a useful length. It is perhaps also worth pointing out the way in which the background is neatly formed by the roadway. This is slightly on an embankment like the prototype and encloses the scene. A few buildings and a few trees have been added to fill in any gaps in the skyline and make the background look more realistic. I am quite pleased by the way it all fell into place, making this still a busy-looking terminus, but one that could be modelled in a small space.

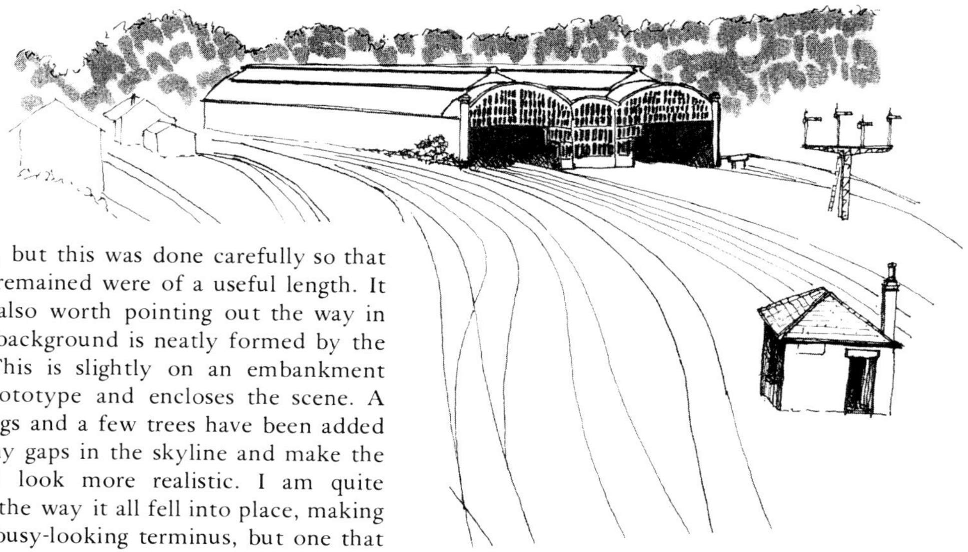

DOLWYDDELAN

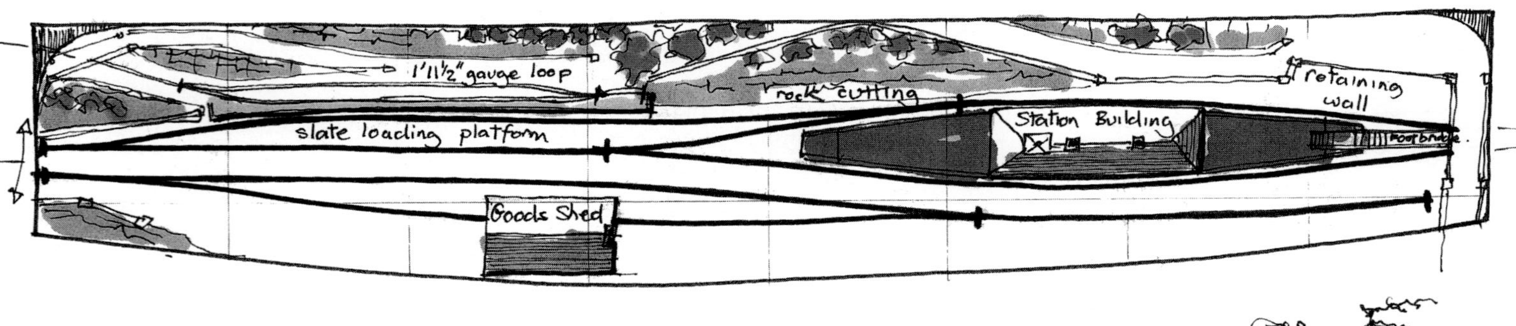

I was looking for a station to fit into a thin and not too long space, such as the side wall of a garage. Clearly, to be narrow, the background would have to gain height in a very short space, and this started me thinking about rock cuttings and retaining walls. Rock cuttings made me think of Wales, so I flicked through my books and came upon Dolwyddelan on the branch line from Blaenau Ffestiniog to Llandudno Junction.

The choice of this station was also influenced by the slate wharf which, as you can see, I have developed rather further than the prototype by adding a narrow gauge line. I thought that this would add to the operational possibilities of the station and help to stamp the character of its location on the layout.

So there you have it, a design decided by a small rock cutting, which coincidentally emphasised the rather fine waiting room and booking office on the island platform, which in itself was something quite different.

WANTAGE

There are small stations, but Wantage must rate as one of the tiniest. This was no doubt due to its cramped site, a stone's throw from the town centre. The tramway built its terminus here amongst the backs of buildings, providing a train shed for the passengers that used to ride the railway in its early days, and engine sheds for its quaint collection of 0–4–0 tank and tram engines. Everything was unusual about this railway, from the tramcar carriages to the roadside track.

I was looking for a prototype that I could model in a display cabinet – Wantage seemed ideal. It was not only small, but had an interesting track layout, enabling an incoming train to be shunted between the goods yard, coal wharf and gasworks. As mentioned, in the earlier days of its history, a passenger platform was also in use (just off the right-hand side of the design).

Scenically, the site was also appealing. The engine shed could be used to block any views of one fiddle yard, and with the presence of the Gas Manager's house and gasworks, the background is taken care of. Each building also had much character, and would make an interesting topic to model – altogether a fascinating scene with considerable detail.

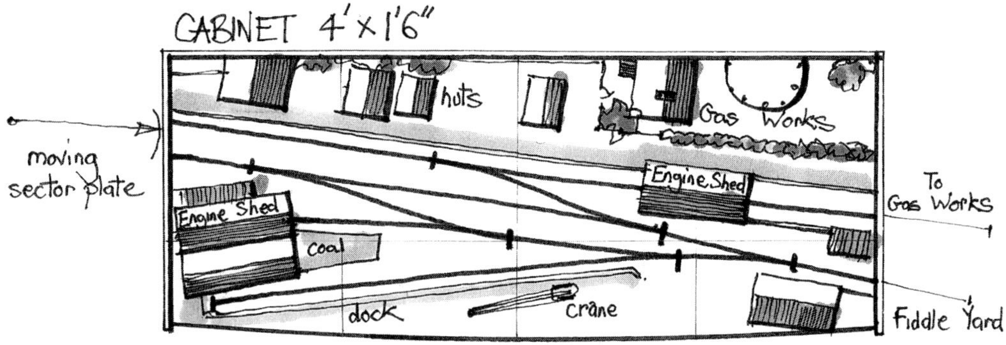

M. F. YARWOOD

RUSPIDGE

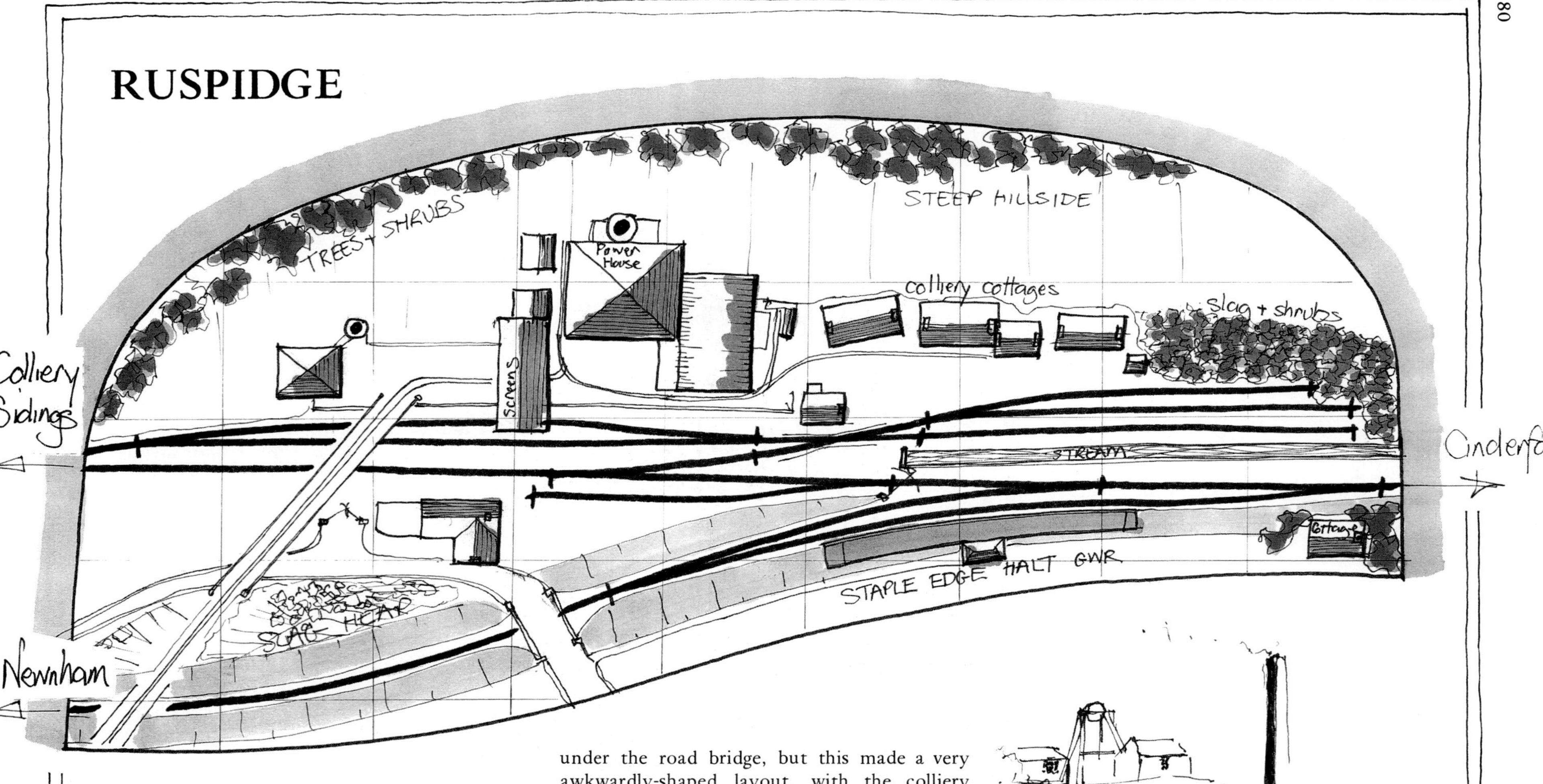

This design, based upon the Eastern United Colliery at Ruspidge, puzzled me for some time and I did several drawings of it until I arrived at one I liked. The difficulty lay in trying to route the Great Western line so that I could see (and reach) the colliery behind. I also had to decide how to end the model so that all the lines could be screened in some way from the fiddle yards. Perhaps looking at this design you may think that the solution seemed obvious – but it wasn't. The branch line should have curved in the opposite direction once it passed under the road bridge, but this made a very awkwardly-shaped layout, with the colliery trapped in a corner. I tried making the scene 'L' shaped – but this didn't work, so I redirected the GW line beneath the spoil tip and used the narrow gauge pit railway as the break. In doing this, the colliery sidings were also screened as they went through the back-scene.

The buildings (wheelhouse, powerhouse, screens and cottages) have much character, and portray a lively industrial scene full of detail and interest. They also create a neat backdrop at the foot of a thickly wooded hillside. This grimy diorama took much thinking about.

REDRU H

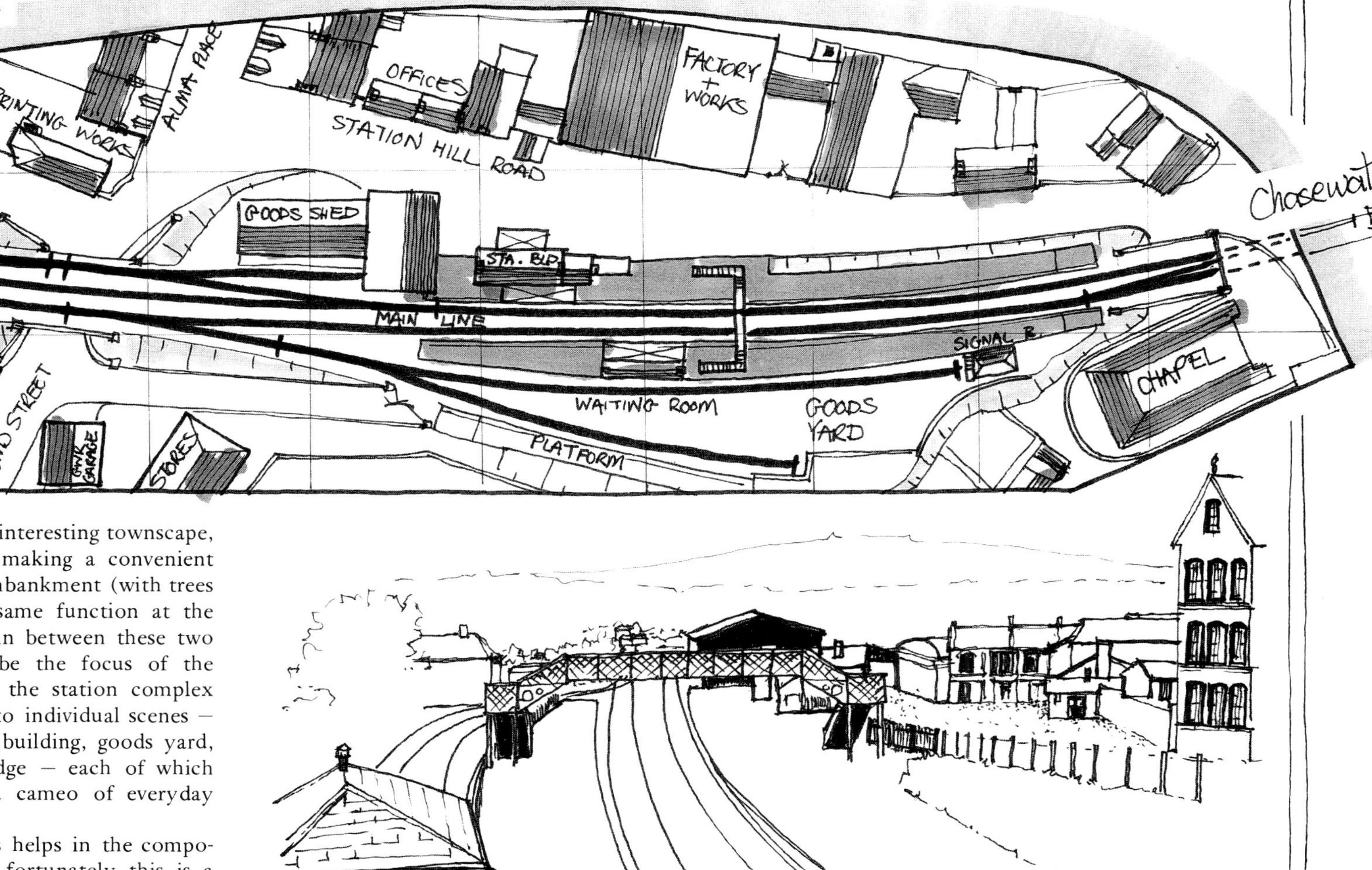

The station sits within an interesting townscape, the chapel at one end making a convenient scenic break, with the embankment (with trees added) performing the same function at the other end. The station in between these two points must obviously be the focus of the whole model. However, the station complex itself is broken down into individual scenes – the goods shed, station building, goods yard, road bridge and footbridge – each of which could be modelled as a cameo of everyday Cornish railway life.

Use of different levels helps in the composition of a model, and fortunately this is a natural feature of this location. High ground by the tunnel falls gradually away, leaving the main line elevated on an embankment. This is useful, as the height of the foreground buildings at the tunnel end can be used to channel some challenging views of the station over the rooftops. As I have already mentioned, it is a good idea to obscure the view of the train, and these buildings help to do this. At the other end of the layout they also funnel one's vision under the arch of Bond Street bridge, creating a glimpse of Station Hill, Alma Place and the printing works beyond.

The background needs to break the skyline and this is not difficult to achieve here with so many buildings behind the station. I can imagine watching a Great Western 'Bulldog' wrapped in steam emerging from the tunnel and into the station. A clatter of signal arms and it will be off again with wheels squealing as it rounds the curve out of the station and across the embankment. When layouts are planned, like this example, with only 10ft to play with, much thought has to be put into the project. The placing of scenes and views would enhance the prototype and the many cameos that can be created in this design prompt thoughts of Ditchling Green. It would make a 7mm scale layout of only 18ft in length.

This Welsh design divides into three distinct scenes – Abergynolwyn station, the winding drum house and Alltwyllt sorting sidings. No one of these components singly could have made for a very interesting layout, but together the scenic interest and operating potential is greatly enhanced. The problem of limited operation inherent in the typical narrow gauge prototype, with its small, simple stations, is here solved by the composite design. Whilst this design takes obvious liberties with prototype practice, I did not want to stray too far from an actual plan, and the end of the Talyllyn Railway which I chose lent itself very well to this kind of adaption.

Clearly the layout is designed to be viewed from the outside. This is logical as the railway at Abergynolwyn clings to a hillside and this really is the only view possible. Also the curvature of the line out of the station enabled me to turn the layout into a fully scenic circle. I like this, as you can fit a tremendous amount of railway into a small space if it is wound around itself – 30ft in this case. To enable this to happen, the line runs uphill towards Alltwyllt so that a swinging track beneath it at that point can direct trains from Abergynolwyn station into the fiddle yard. This is a design in 7mm (my first choice for narrow gauge) which allows different operation at Alltwyllt incline, sorting sidings, winding drum and station, each forming a scene in its own right.

ABERGYNOLWYN

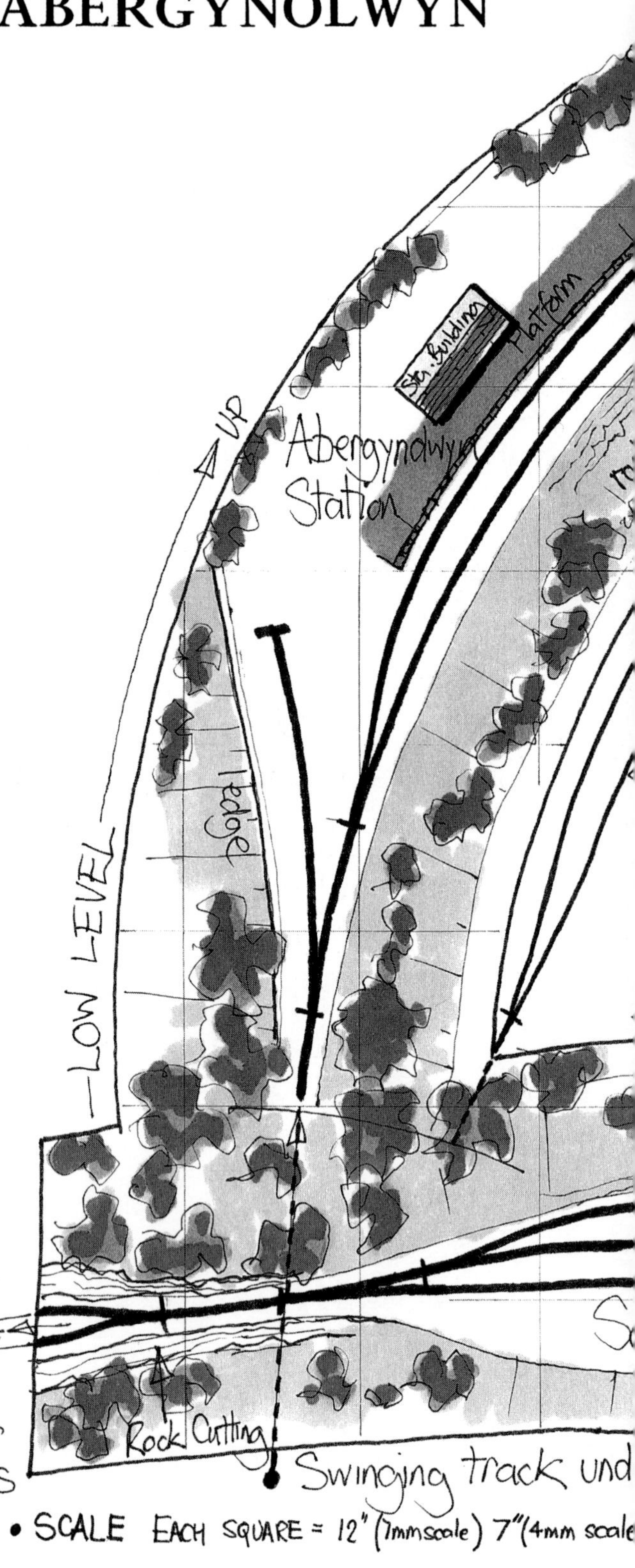

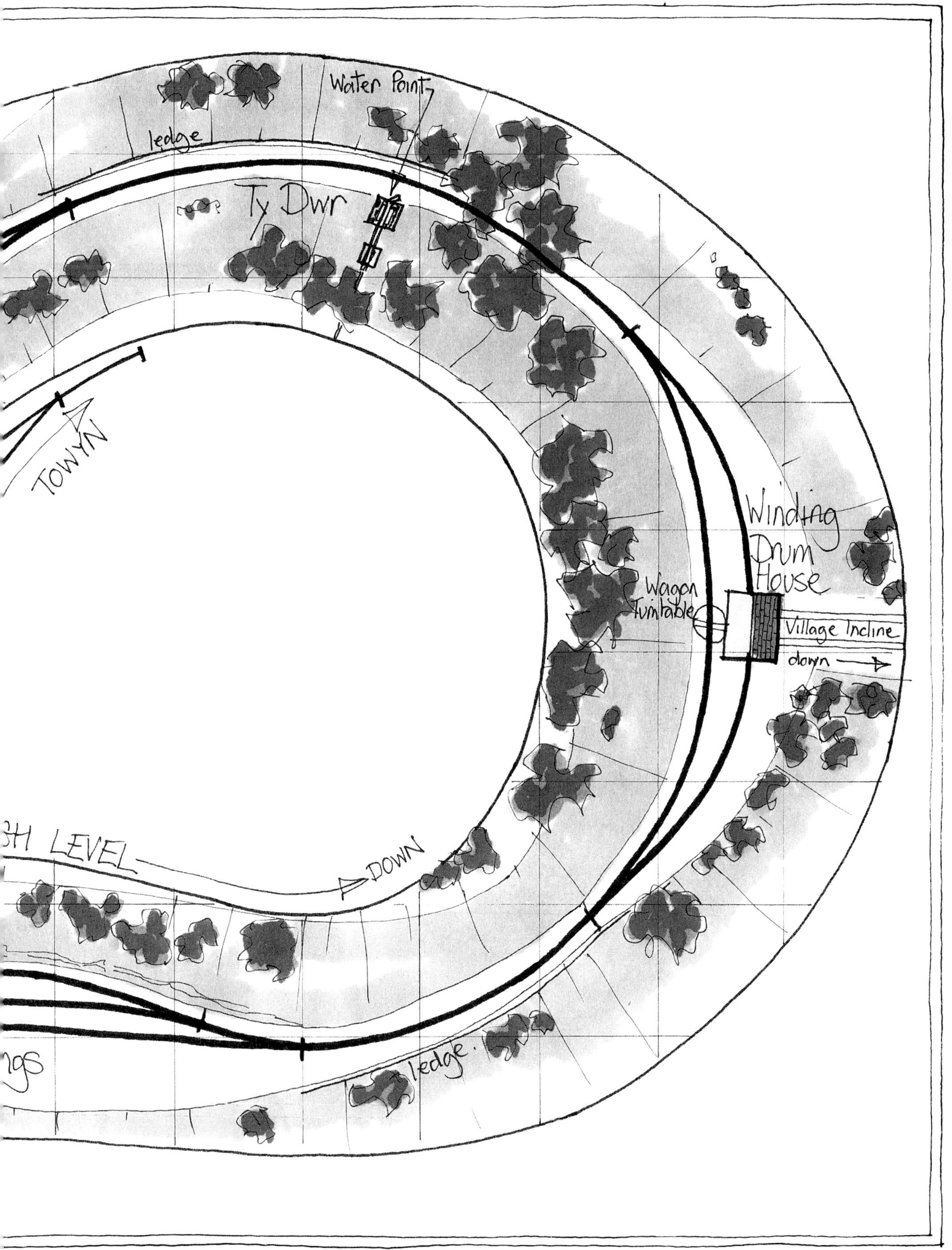
Water Point
ledge
Ty Dwr
TOWYN
Winding
Drum
House
Wagon
Turntable
Village Incline
down
GH LEVEL
DOWN
ledge
ngs

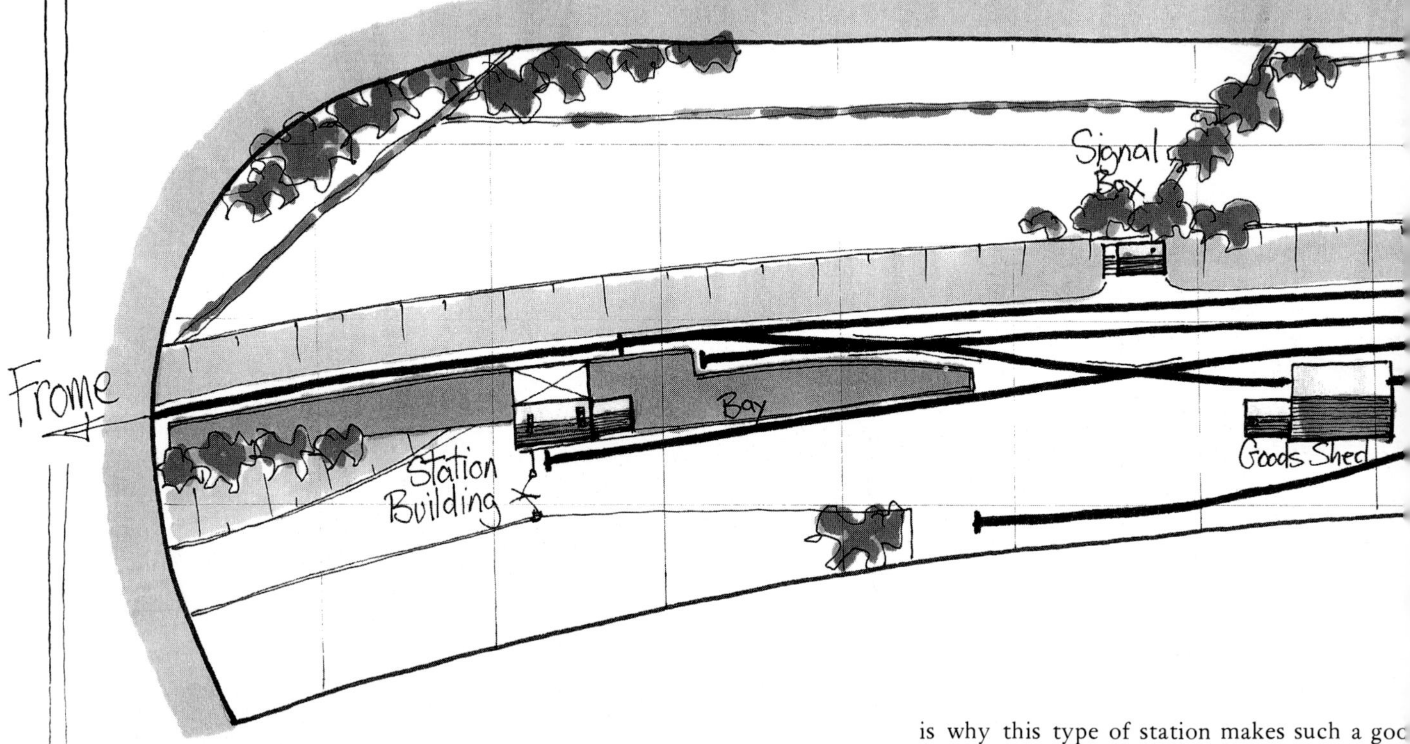

The track plan is simple but sufficiently extensive to deal with the goods, passenger, coal and quarry trains that arrived at the station. Goods train running between Bristol and Frome would stop, shunt off a few wagons and pick up others, many of which had been brought from the Camerton branch goods. Similarly, the branch passenger train would wait and meet the local service from Frome. It might even collect a parcels van from the front of the Bristol train. Threaded in between the day-to-day running of trains would be the shunting of the stone wagons brought down from the quarry. Trains of these would have to be assembled ready to be picked up by a passing goods. Likewise wagons filled with coal would be brought down from the colliery at Camerton and these would have to find their way towards markets in Bristol. This interchange of wagons from one line to another and the diversity of operation is the very essence of a junction station and that is why this type of station makes such a goo model.

Here is a complicated [but simple?] layou It is an immensely attractive station with tir stone buildings set in rolling hills lined wi trees, and a delicate collection of ringed ar and lower quadrant signals – as Great Weste as one can find.

HALLATROW

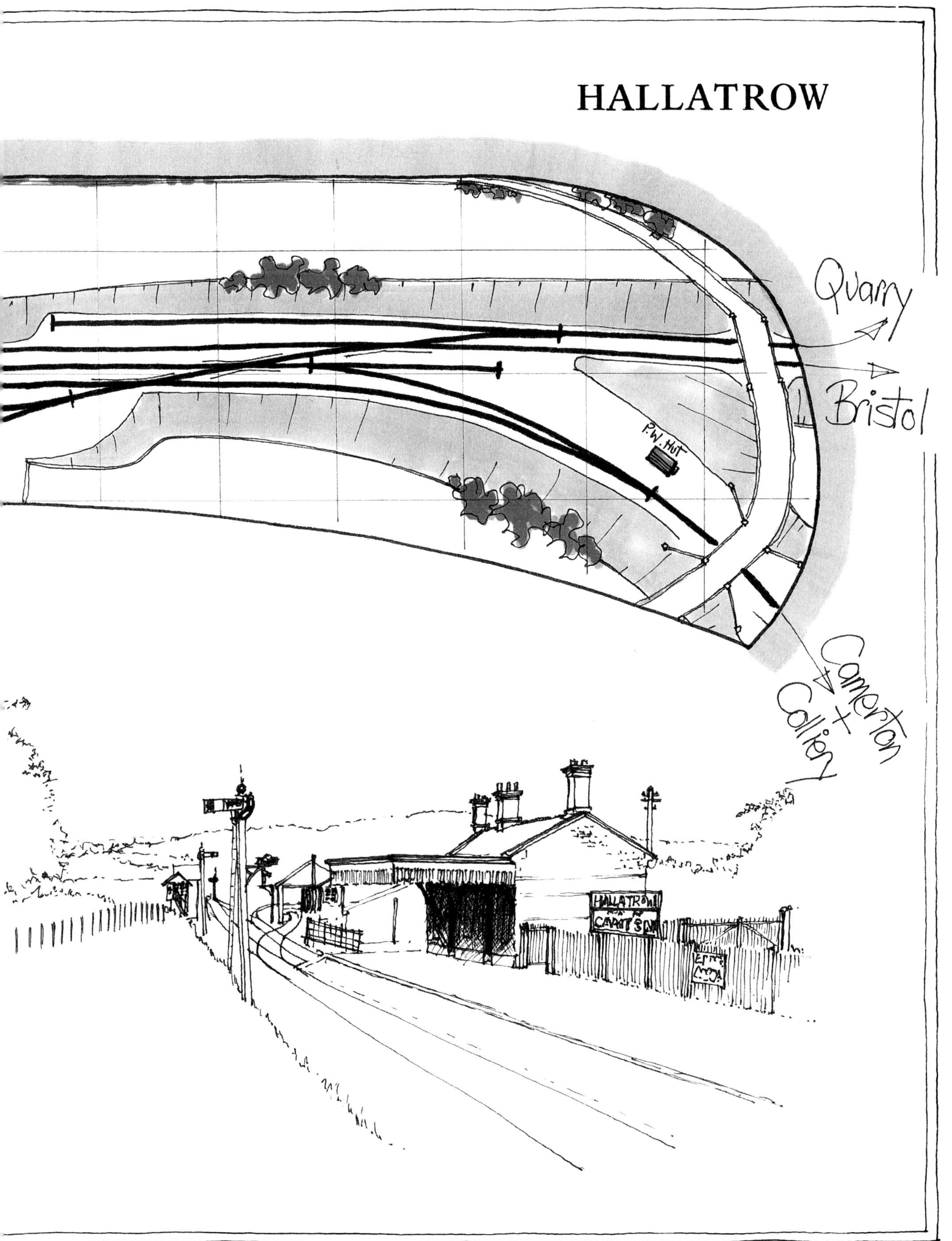

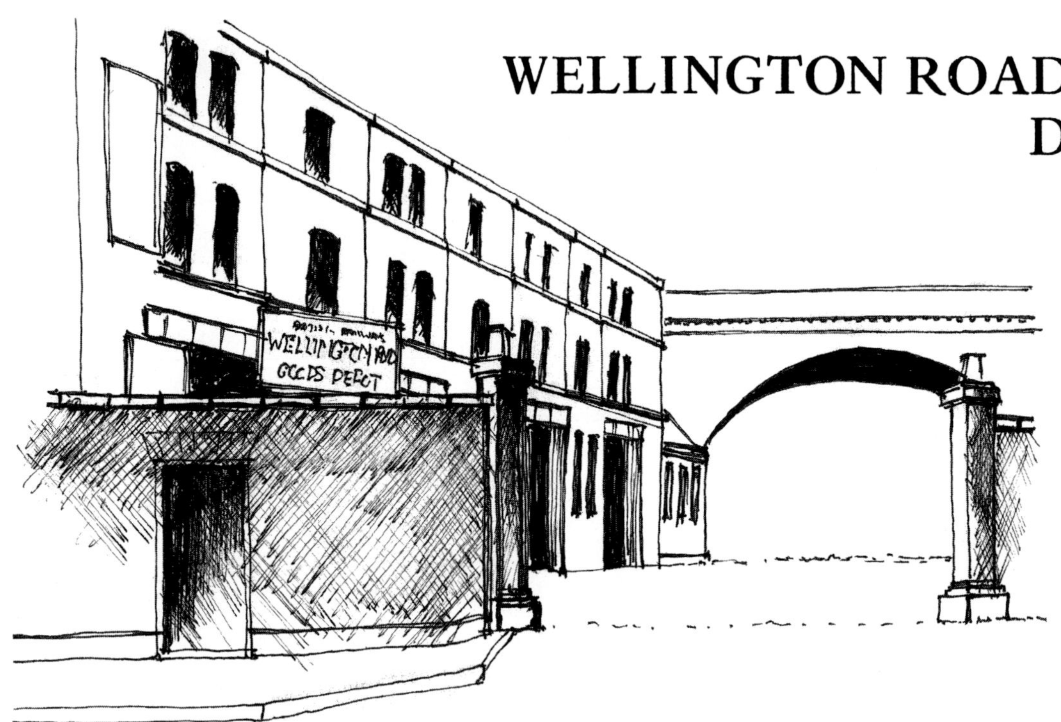

WELLINGTON ROAD GOODS DEPOT

A short distance from Heaton Norris station, the quadruple tracks of the LNWR main line crossed over Wellington Road Goods Depot. For some reason, a few sidings of the large coal yard, built by the Cheshire Lines Committee, were extended through the Stockport viaduct to make this unusual scene. Although the depot itself was not large, its central feature, the warehouse, was a robust-looking three-storey brick structure and rather dominated the yard.

I chose this prototype because I wanted to design a very small minimum-space layout. These have become very popular lately, and I had become very impressed by John Spencer's Ruyton Road. Although small, it oozes with atmosphere and, despite its size, has plenty of scope for shunting. It is perhaps surprising that Wellington Road Goods Depot even existed, but its cramped site offered me just what I was looking for. I have added a turnout to the front

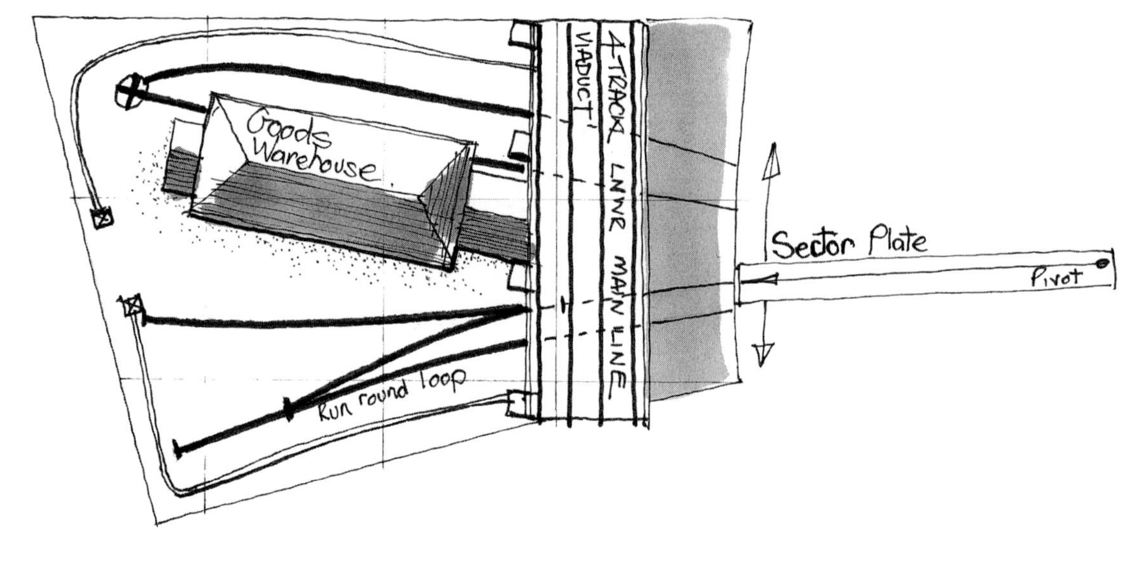

siding to make it one end of a loop so that it would be possible to draw a train into the yard, run round it, and pick off wagons to shunt into the trio of sidings. Conveniently, the mass of the viaduct acts very well as a scenic break and separates the offstage movements on the fiddle yard from the model.

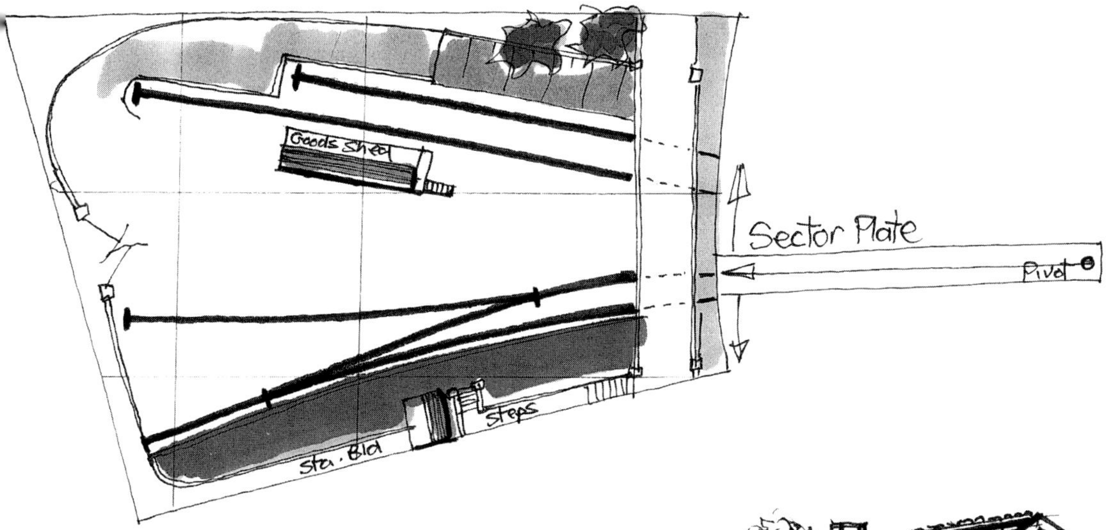

This is a city scene where blackened bricks cast a dismal spell over the railway. It may not be welcoming, but we can't always model the pretty. However, this plan is not without other interpretations. I have, within the same space and to the same track layout, changed the scenery to suit the portrayal of a light railway in the countryside, but there could be many more themes. Interestingly, the goods depot became a scrap yard in its later years, which conjures up an image in my mind of a Peckett saddle tank, wheezing its way through a tangle of iron and steel, with a couple of very beaten three-plank wagons – in 7mm scale!

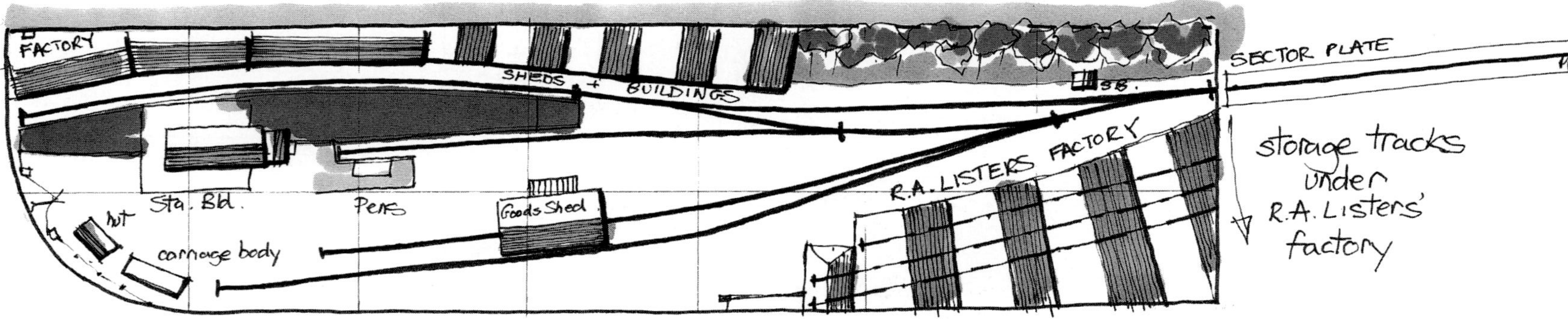

DURSLEY

This former Midland Railway branch line left the Gloucester main line at Coaley Junction. It connected with several mills on its journey to Dursley, culminating in Lister's factory which completely engulfed the station. This was quite an unusual scenario, its uniqueness making the station fascinating to model.

The collection of wooden sheds and brick warehouses that formed part of Lister's engineering business, seemed ideally placed to make a backdrop to this layout. Modelling buildings in half relief is a very space-saving way of creating a backscene, and this prototype lends itself well to this kind of modelling. Good use could also be made of the buildings in the foreground. Clearly they are perfectly positioned to block the view of the fiddle yard and can be adapted to cover the storage tracks that are fed by the sector plate.

As this design developed, the industrial nature of the station became more obvious. R. A. Lister gave this Midland station a character and personality of its own, and it is prudent to capitalize on it. However, within the grip of this manufacturing enterprise, lies a small station of architectural note, reflecting a local style that was slightly Elizabethan in influence. There was the usual goods yard, sidings and docks, but all of this was eased into a very modest space that would suit 7mm scale or 4mm scale.

SELSEY

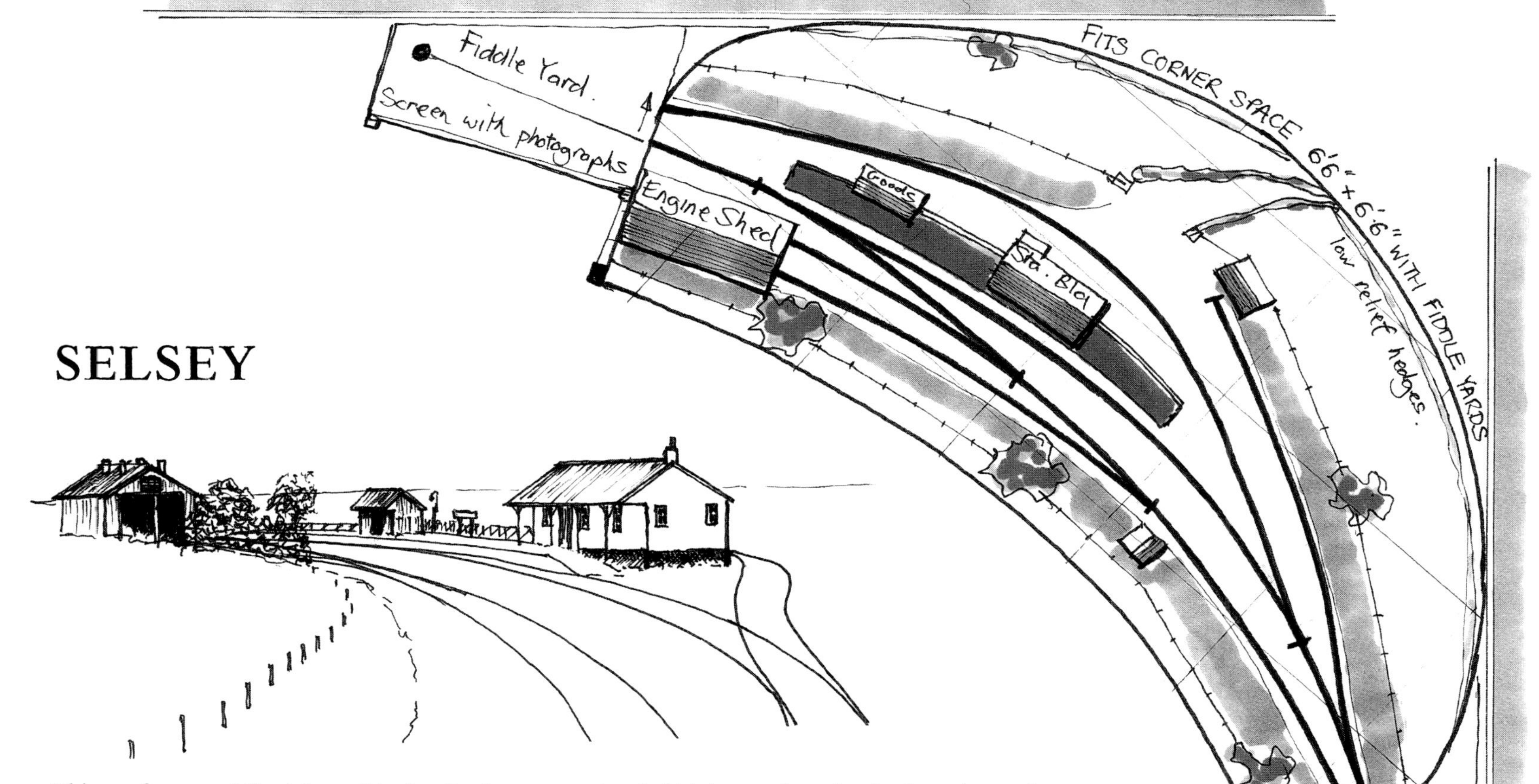

Whisps of steam drifted from *Ringing Rock* as it stood outside the engine shed at Selsey. Inside, another Manning Wardle, probably *Sidlesham*, lay still, with its smokebox door wedged open. Soot had blown on to its slender footplate and the once greased buffers were rusting through neglect. It was a captivating scene overflowing with atmosphere, and one that I thought ought to be at the centre of a model. I found out more about the station and the Hundred of Manhood and Selsey Tramway and realized, not surprisingly, that this was one of Colonel Stephens' family of lines.

That engine shed clad in corrugated iron, was placed in the foreground, neatly to one side so that it hid the moving of trains in and out of the Fiddle Yard. It also balanced the similarly clad station building, and set the tone to the atmosphere of the whole diorama.

I chose to curve the running line more fully into 90° so that I could place the design into the corner of a room. In this way it was possible to fill a comparatively small space with more than if the station had been stretched into a straight line and placed against one wall. This thoughtful use of space is another practical way of finding a home for a small but interesting layout.

From the station forecourt, the cobbled approach road fell downhill and left the platforms high above on a ledge. The ornate train shed overlooked the sheer brick retaining wall that hugged the road, and spanned the bay platforms. Shortly the whole scene was to become a medley of bridges that crossed the Mersey on different levels. From each, one could look back into the waters that were flowing far beneath the railway.

Mills and factories rose from the river banks and peered over the double-tracked main line as it widened into its quadruple tracks. This industrial landscape through which the line winds, encloses Tiviot Dale in a backcloth of distant chimneys and cotton mills. It surrounds the scene and rises towards the station building on Lancashire Hill as it crosses the railway and passes the Hanover Chapel. In the other direction, Stockport Mills clings precariously to the river embankment and shelters the railway.

Thus Tiviot Dale emerges as an ideal layout. Operationally, there is considerable scope for

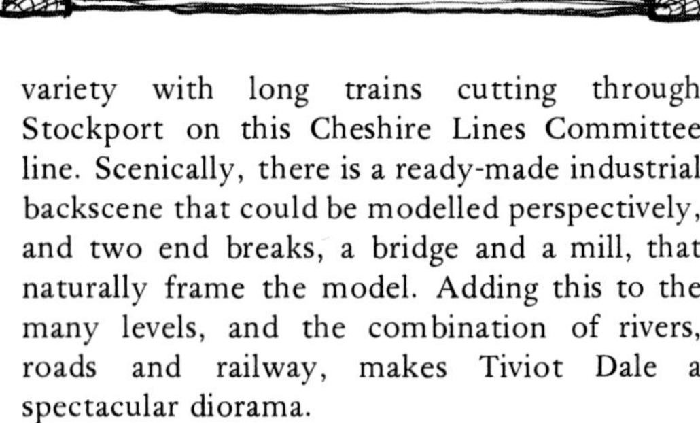

variety with long trains cutting through Stockport on this Cheshire Lines Committee line. Scenically, there is a ready-made industrial backscene that could be modelled perspectively, and two end breaks, a bridge and a mill, that naturally frame the model. Adding this to the many levels, and the combination of rivers, roads and railway, makes Tiviot Dale a spectacular diorama.

I have designed this in only 8 feet by placing the layout within a shed. In this way it is possible to wind the return loops back under the station to a fiddle yard. We have continuous running in a space 8ft by 6ft – work out how big a room would be needed in your house!

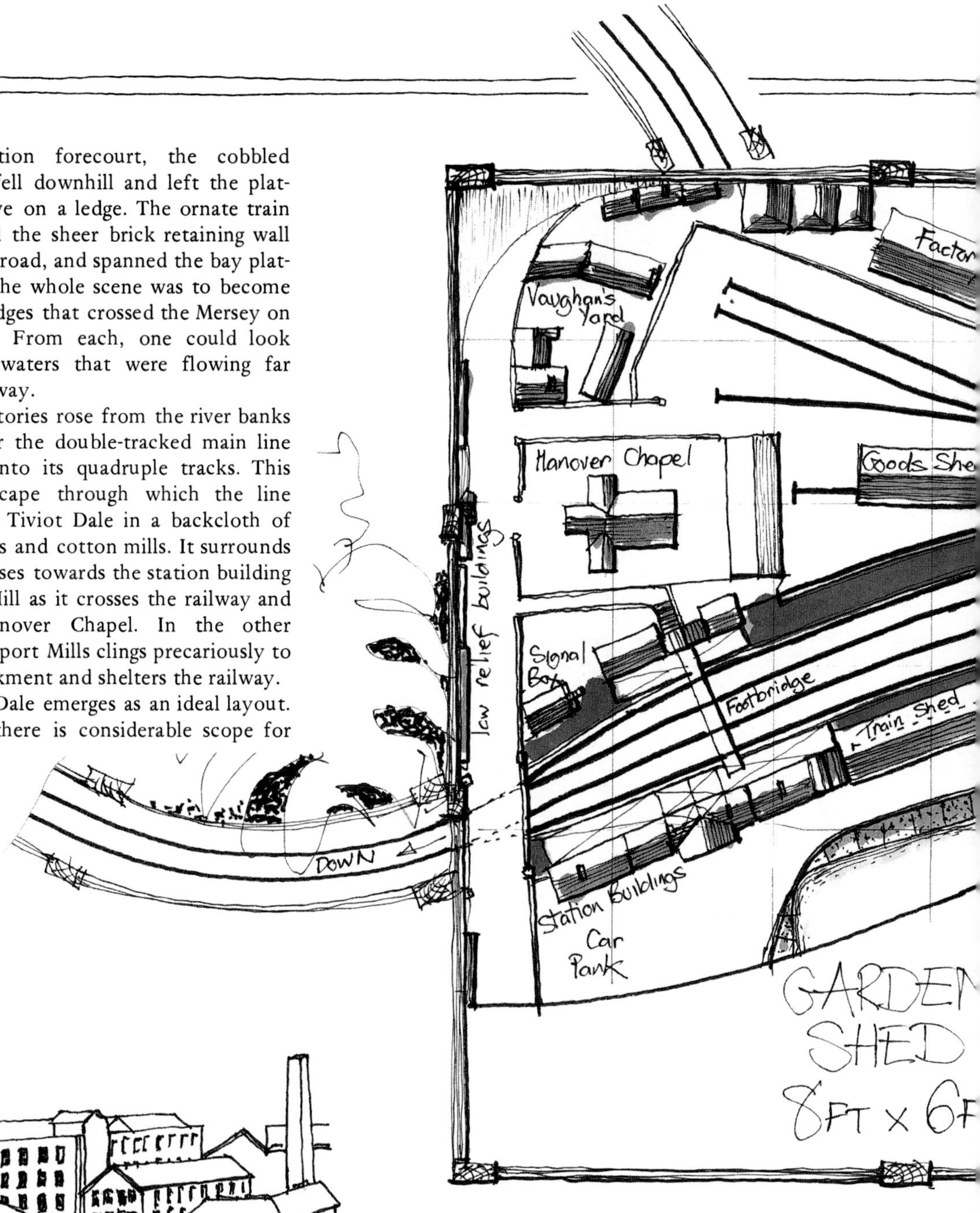

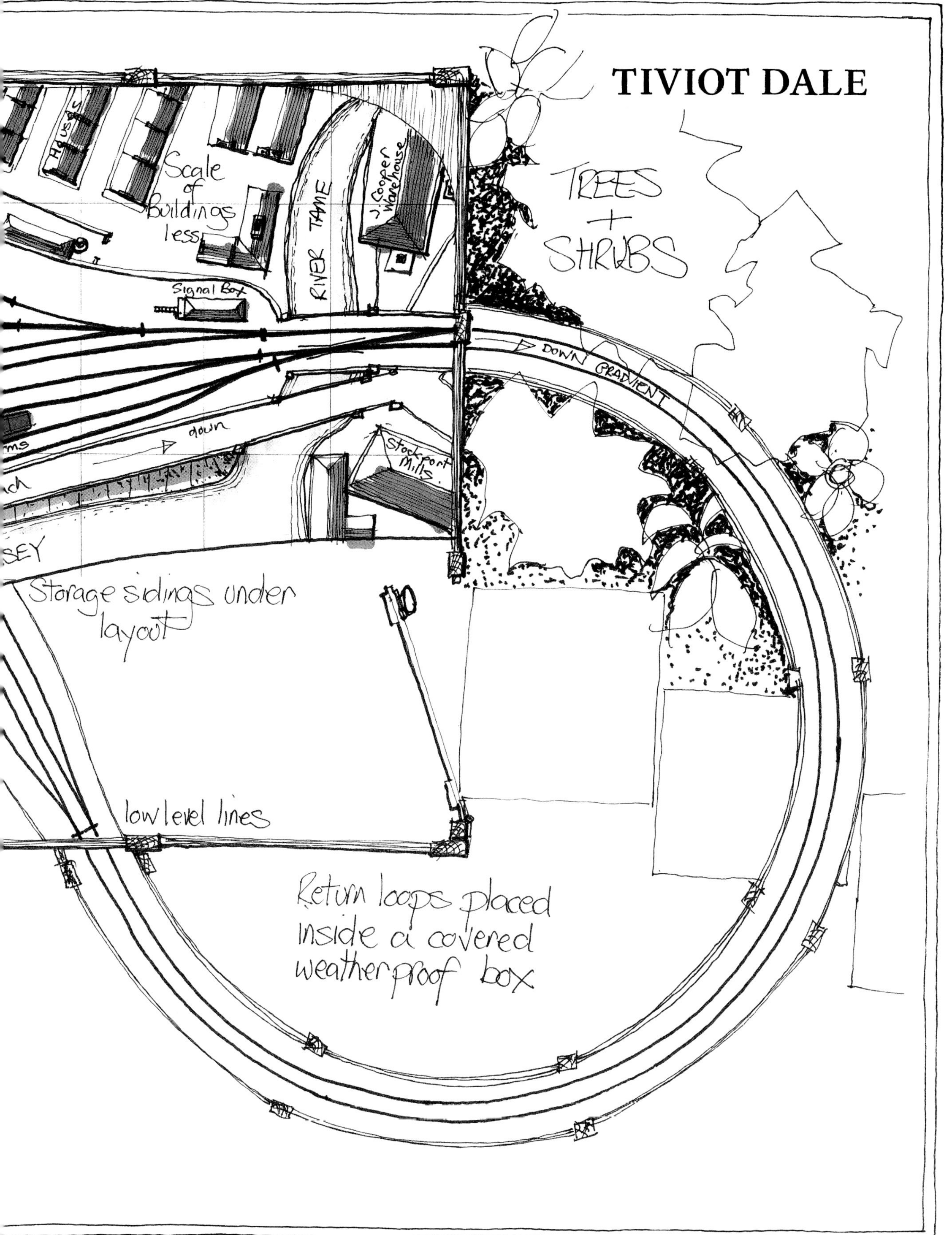
TIVIOT DALE
TREES + SHRUBS
Houses
Scale of Buildings less
J. Cooper Warehouse
RIVER TAME
Signal Box
DOWN GRADIENT
down
Stockport Mills
SEY
Storage sidings under layout
low level lines
Return loops placed inside a covered weatherproof box

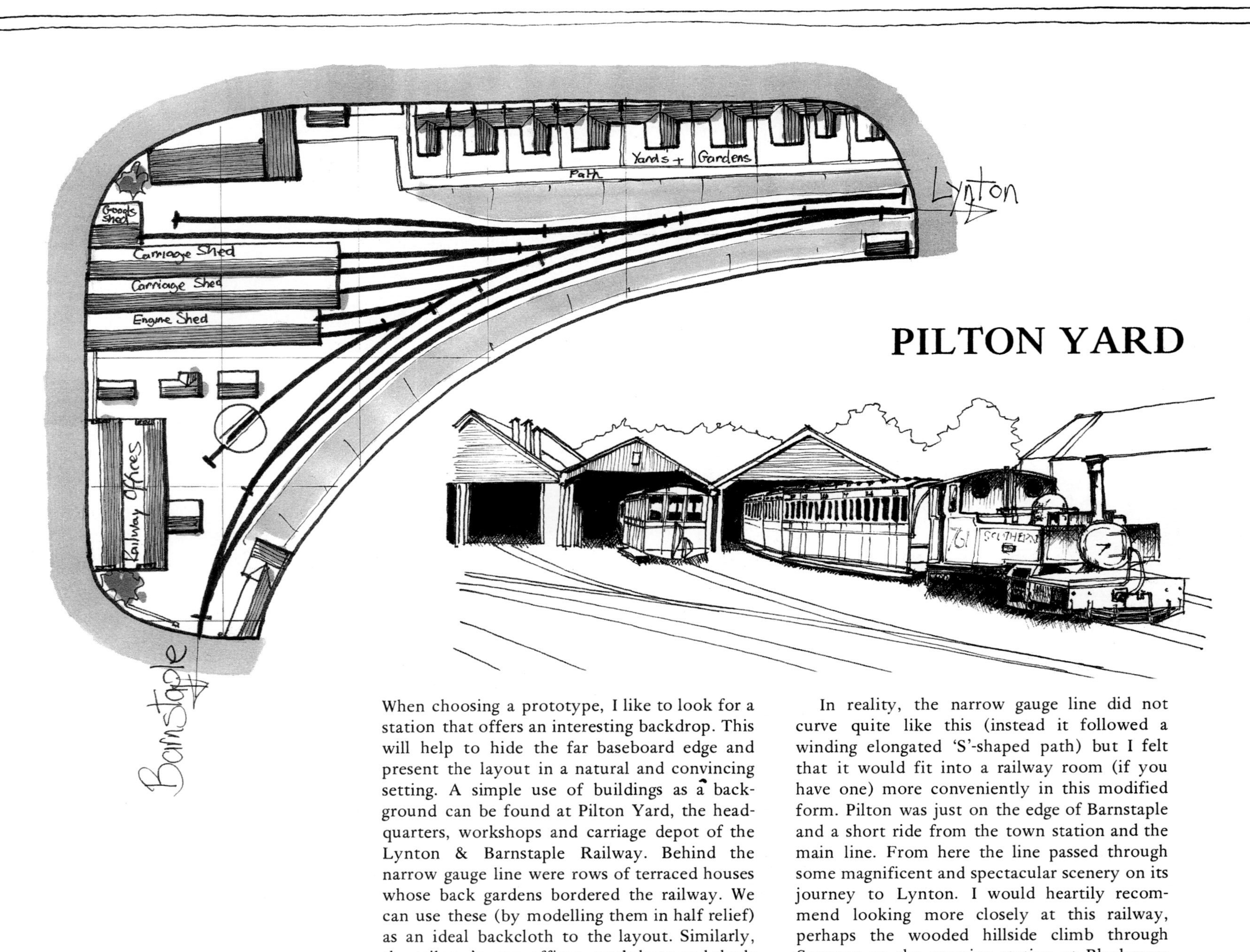

PILTON YARD

When choosing a prototype, I like to look for a station that offers an interesting backdrop. This will help to hide the far baseboard edge and present the layout in a natural and convincing setting. A simple use of buildings as a background can be found at Pilton Yard, the headquarters, workshops and carriage depot of the Lynton & Barnstaple Railway. Behind the narrow gauge line were rows of terraced houses whose back gardens bordered the railway. We can use these (by modelling them in half relief) as an ideal backcloth to the layout. Similarly, the railway's own offices, workshops and sheds may be used to screen off the other side of the

In reality, the narrow gauge line did not curve quite like this (instead it followed a winding elongated 'S'-shaped path) but I felt that it would fit into a railway room (if you have one) more conveniently in this modified form. Pilton was just on the edge of Barnstaple and a short ride from the town station and the main line. From here the line passed through some magnificent and spectacular scenery on its journey to Lynton. I would heartily recommend looking more closely at this railway, perhaps the wooded hillside climb through Snapper or the crossing station at Blackmore Gate with its Swiss-styled chalet buildings. It

Sometimes, as in this design based upon Loch Tay, I am really left wondering how best to present the plan. I liked the scenic hillside location, but the line curving towards the pier was the problem. I did think about making the layout 'L' shaped, but this would leave a rather awkward area to fill behind the goods yard and make the background difficult to disguise. I wanted to make the pier (surrounded by as much of the Loch as possible) the central feature of the layout, and thought of ways of emphasising this. As can be seen, I chose to wind the front edge around the pier and goods yard. This allowed me to retain close contact with the goods yard (for uncoupling when shunting) and created views of the pier from three sides. This was important as I always had in my mind's eye the scene of a string of wagons waiting for a tank engine to run round them, all reflected in the rippling water beneath.

I also decided to add a few sidings to the goods yard to make the station more interesting to operate, but I was very careful to retain the intimate nature of this station and preserve its Scottish flavour. For me, this is an exciting layout. The unusual shape is interesting to look at, but is entirely practical. The background is neatly retained by a simply curving hillside that rises above the station, and the front twists and winds the eye around the model, taking in enough of the Loch to emphasise the importance of the water's edge.

LOCH TAY

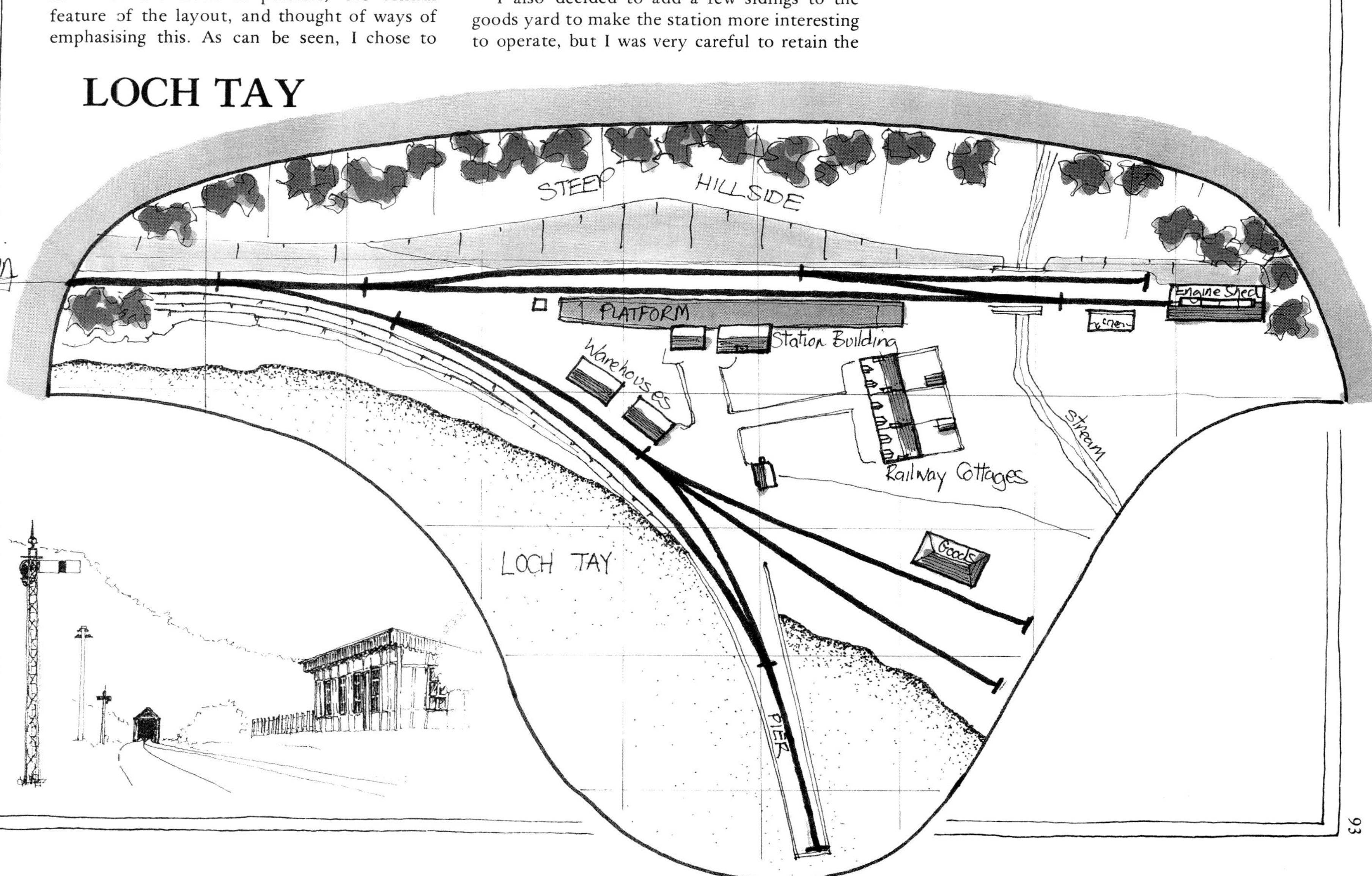

Another kind of junction station was found at Charwelton. This was the meeting place of two quite different railways: the ex-GCR main line between Rugby and Woodford Halse, and the industrial Charwelton Ironstone railway. Here was a marked contrast of styles. Twelve-coach expresses would have roared through the station followed by long winding freight trains, whilst a small industrial saddle tank would be shunting the loaded mineral wagons it had just brought from the quarry. Operation and action are keynotes of this design, all squeezed into a room 12ft x 8ft.

I can imagine opening the door and slipping into the railway room, sitting down and ringing a 3:1 through to the signal box at Charwelton and waiting for a B1 with ten carmine and cream Mark I carriages to leave Catesby tunnel. The excitement of main-line running is a major feature of this plan. Perhaps the 'Master Cutler' would pass under the station road bridge and rush by the small brick platform buildings that were such a unique feature of Great Central stations.

In this design the track plan has been shortened somewhat, but the relationship between the main line and ironstone railway is preserved. This is an important feature of the plan, expecially in the way the industrial line runs off away from the station, past its engine shed and under the main-line fiddle yard. Like Hallatrow, this is a plan where operational interest does not mean yards and yards of track, just an intelligent use of a little.

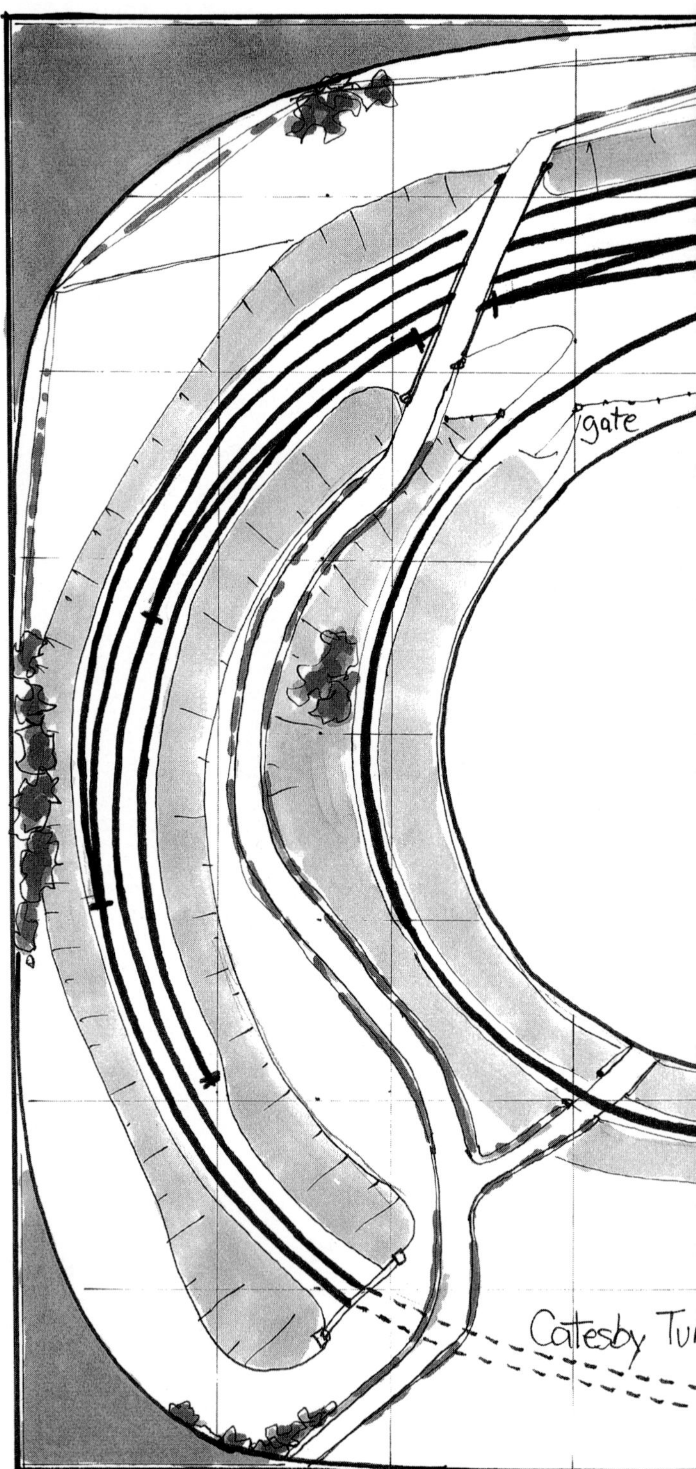

CHARWELTON

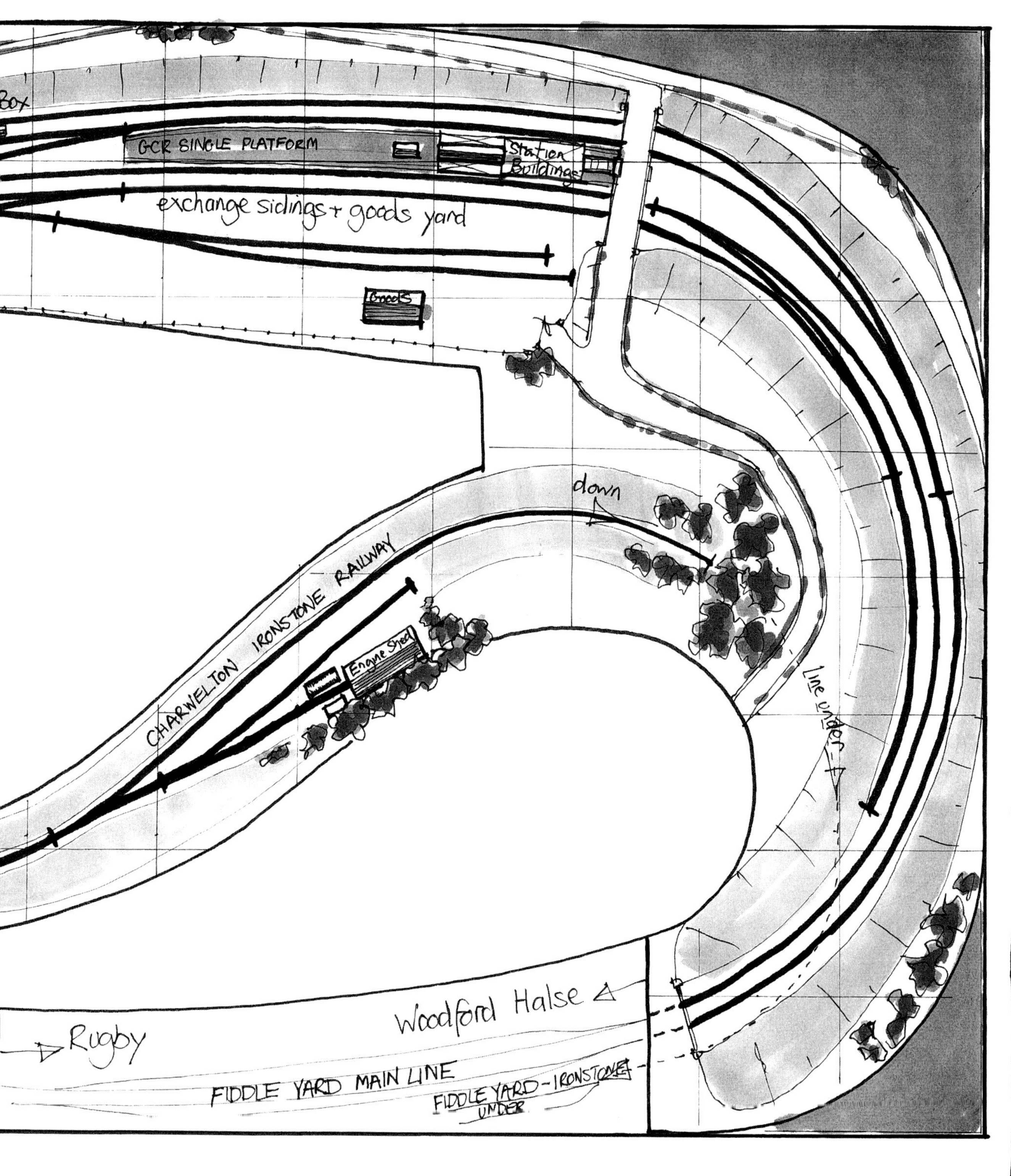
Box
GCR SINGLE PLATFORM
Station Buildings
exchange sidings + goods yard
Goods
down
CHARWELTON IRONSTONE RAILWAY
Engine Shed
Line under
Woodford Halse
Rugby
FIDDLE YARD MAIN LINE
FIDDLE YARD - IRONSTONE UNDER

LYMINGE

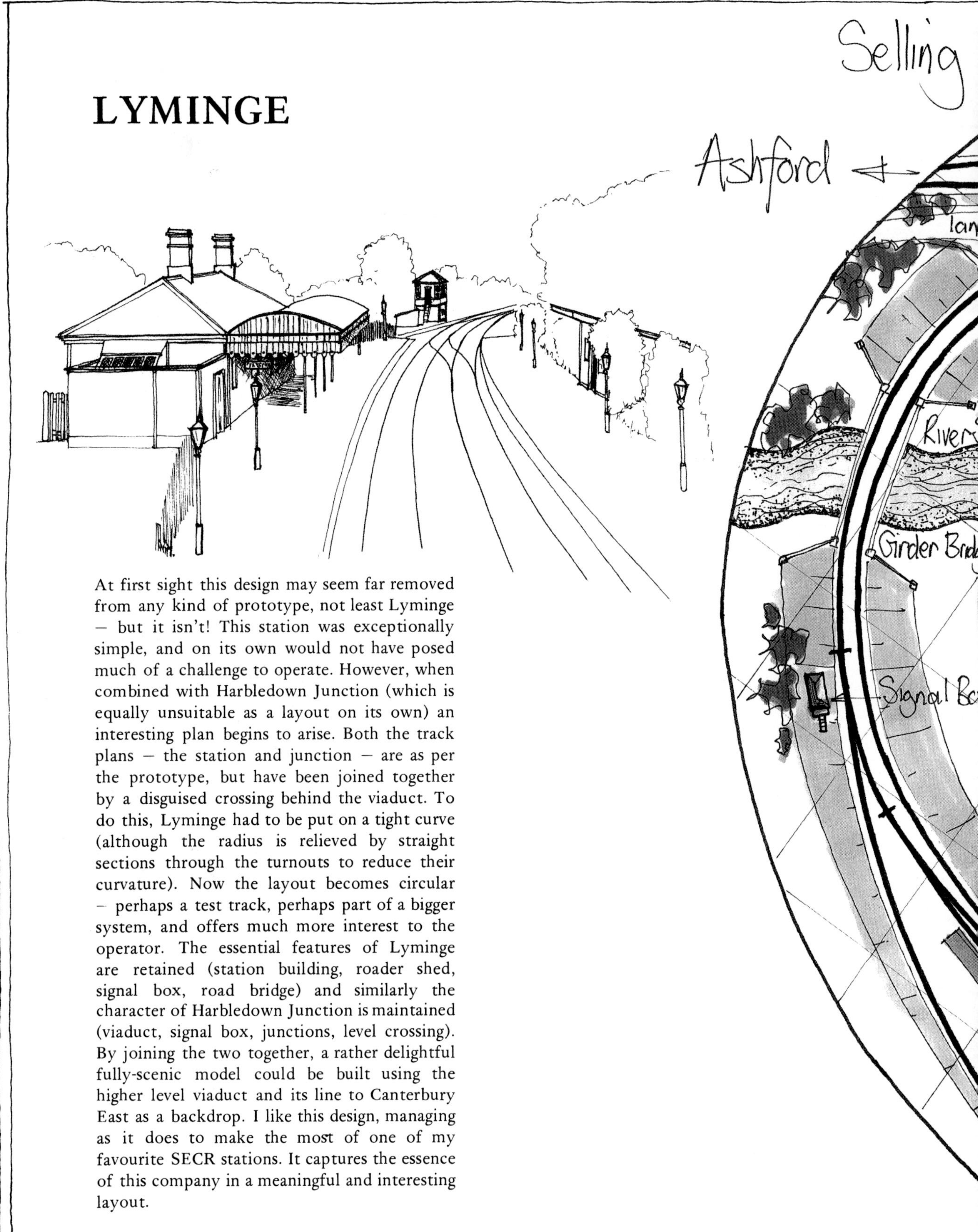

At first sight this design may seem far removed from any kind of prototype, not least Lyminge — but it isn't! This station was exceptionally simple, and on its own would not have posed much of a challenge to operate. However, when combined with Harbledown Junction (which is equally unsuitable as a layout on its own) an interesting plan begins to arise. Both the track plans — the station and junction — are as per the prototype, but have been joined together by a disguised crossing behind the viaduct. To do this, Lyminge had to be put on a tight curve (although the radius is relieved by straight sections through the turnouts to reduce their curvature). Now the layout becomes circular – perhaps a test track, perhaps part of a bigger system, and offers much more interest to the operator. The essential features of Lyminge are retained (station building, roader shed, signal box, road bridge) and similarly the character of Harbledown Junction is maintained (viaduct, signal box, junctions, level crossing). By joining the two together, a rather delightful fully-scenic model could be built using the higher level viaduct and its line to Canterbury East as a backdrop. I like this design, managing as it does to make the most of one of my favourite SECR stations. It captures the essence of this company in a meaningful and interesting layout.

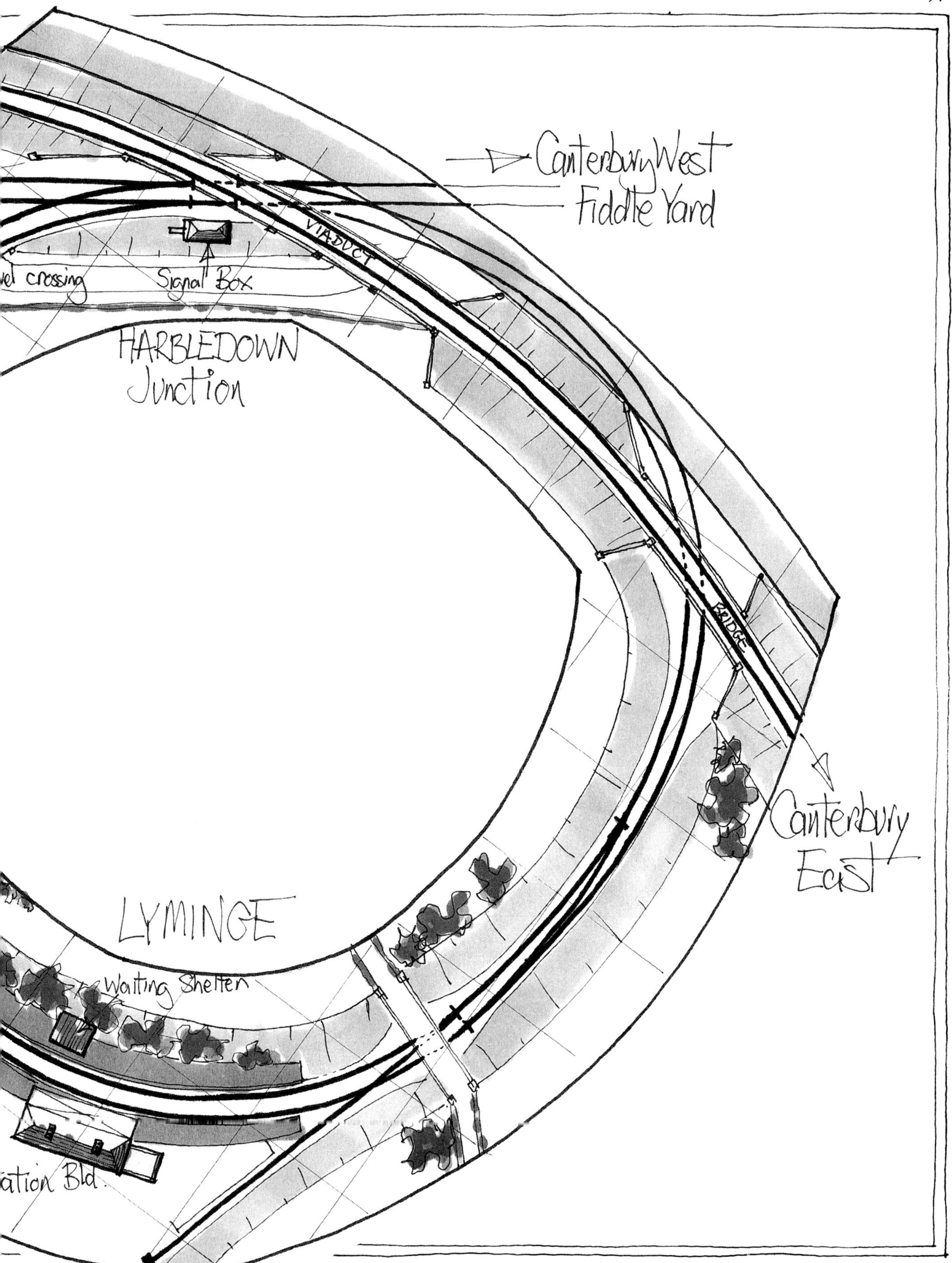
Canterbury West
Fiddle Yard
VIADUCT
Signal Box
crossing
HARBLEDOWN
Junction
BRIDGE
Canterbury
East
LYMINGE
Waiting Shelter
ation Bld.

ALDEBURGH

Aldeburgh rests at the end of a Great Eastern branch line within sight of the sea. Although a small station, it was long, so I felt I needed to make some alterations. Trackwise there is some shortening of the sidings and the final turnout into the goods yard has been replaced by the fiddle yard. However, the essence of the plan has been retained, as have all the buildings, including the rather wonderful train shed and station building. The most obvious change is without doubt the road bridge which I felt I needed to add to the design. A real difficulty when working on East Anglian settings is the flatness of the landscape which offers few natural ways to lose the fiddle yard from view. Although the road bridge is a rather predictable solution to the problem, I could see no alternative.

I liked the view down the layout from the bridge and could imagine a cloudless Suffolk sky above it, so I decided to make this the focal point of the layout. The bridge with its approach road became the backscene, and the shape of the layout was planned to bring the eye towards this.

MONUMENT LANE

An engine shed is an obvious choice for a layout if you enjoy collecting and building locomotives. However, its potential for operation is rather limited. To overcome this, I have included with the shed the adjoining main line and goods yard. This creates a trio of distinct features, each of which could be operated independently. The sum of these three parts compensates for the limitations of each on its own.

With water tower, coal plant and turntable complementing the six-road shed, Monument Lane was a depot of considerable importance. Likewise the goods yard with its long sidings and large shed could be considered a grand affair, with plenty of work to keep a tank engine busy. Between these, runs the main Birmingham to Wolverhampton line, a major route on which the largest of trains will travel. By adding all this together, it can be seen that this small layout has considerable operational potential, perhaps a good choice for a club or a group.

The problem of background is here solved naturally by the nature of the prototype. To the right the main line disappears into a tunnel and on the left it passes under a road bridge, the two making ideal ways of ending the layout and disguising the fiddle yards. These are the traditional ways of masking the ends of a model and it is surprising to find a prototype that suits so well. Between these, the ground is high, built up on a retaining wall. This supports a road which folds around the scene, successfully breaking the skyline. The addition of a few shops and terraced house ensures that the background naturally separates the model from the sky.

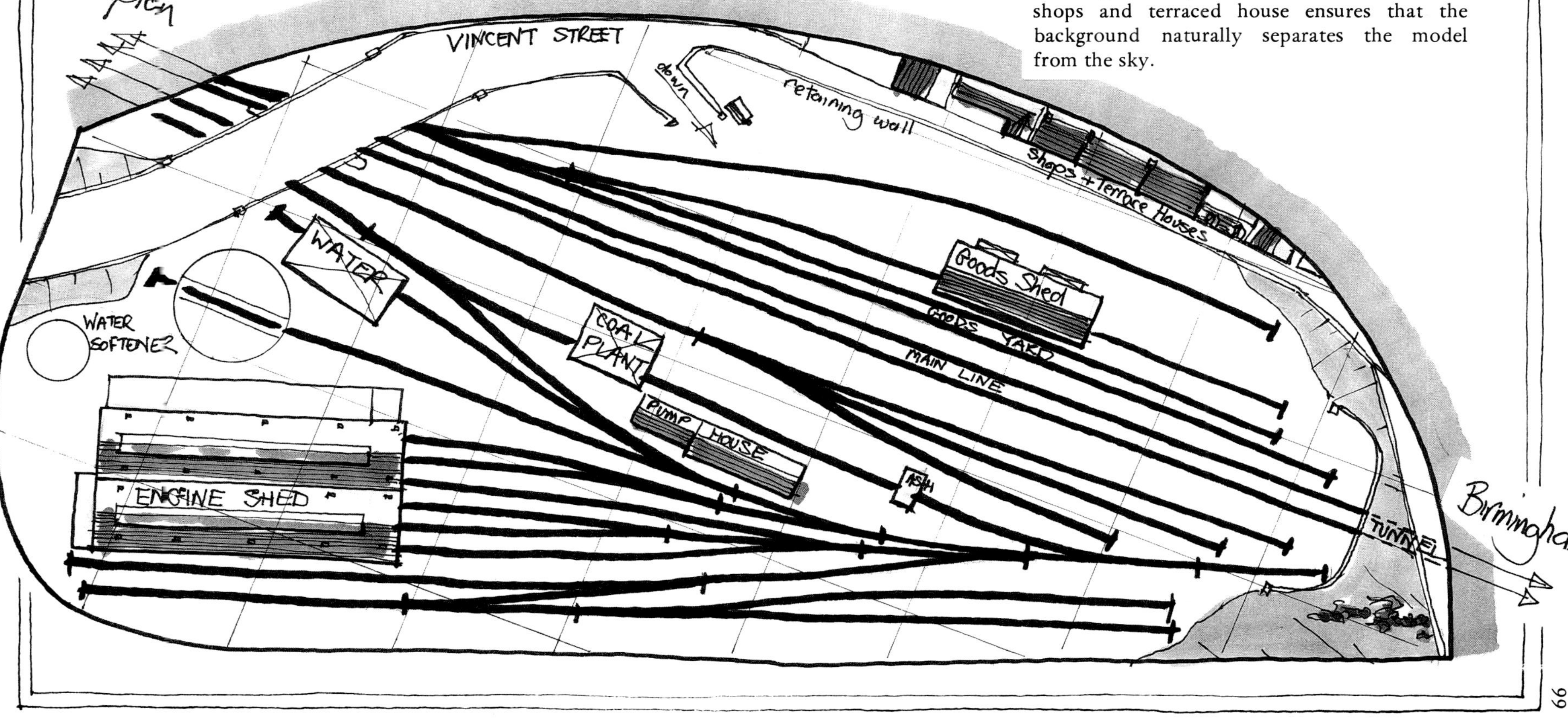

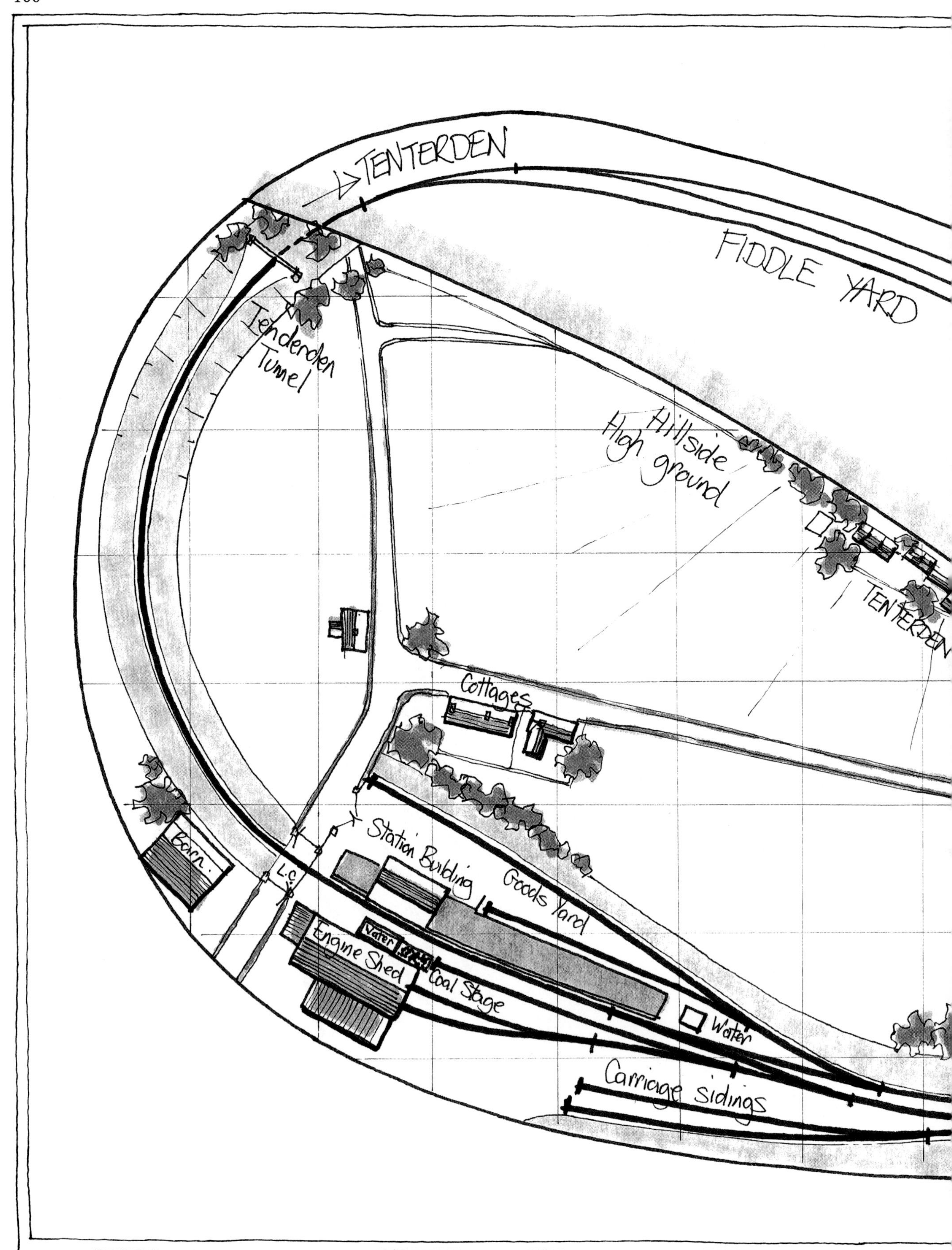
TENTERDEN
FIDDLE YARD
Tenderden Tunnel
Hillside High ground
TENTERDEN
Cottages
Station Building
Goods Yard
Barn.
L.C.
Water
Engine Shed
Coal Stage
Water
Carriage sidings

ROLVENDEN

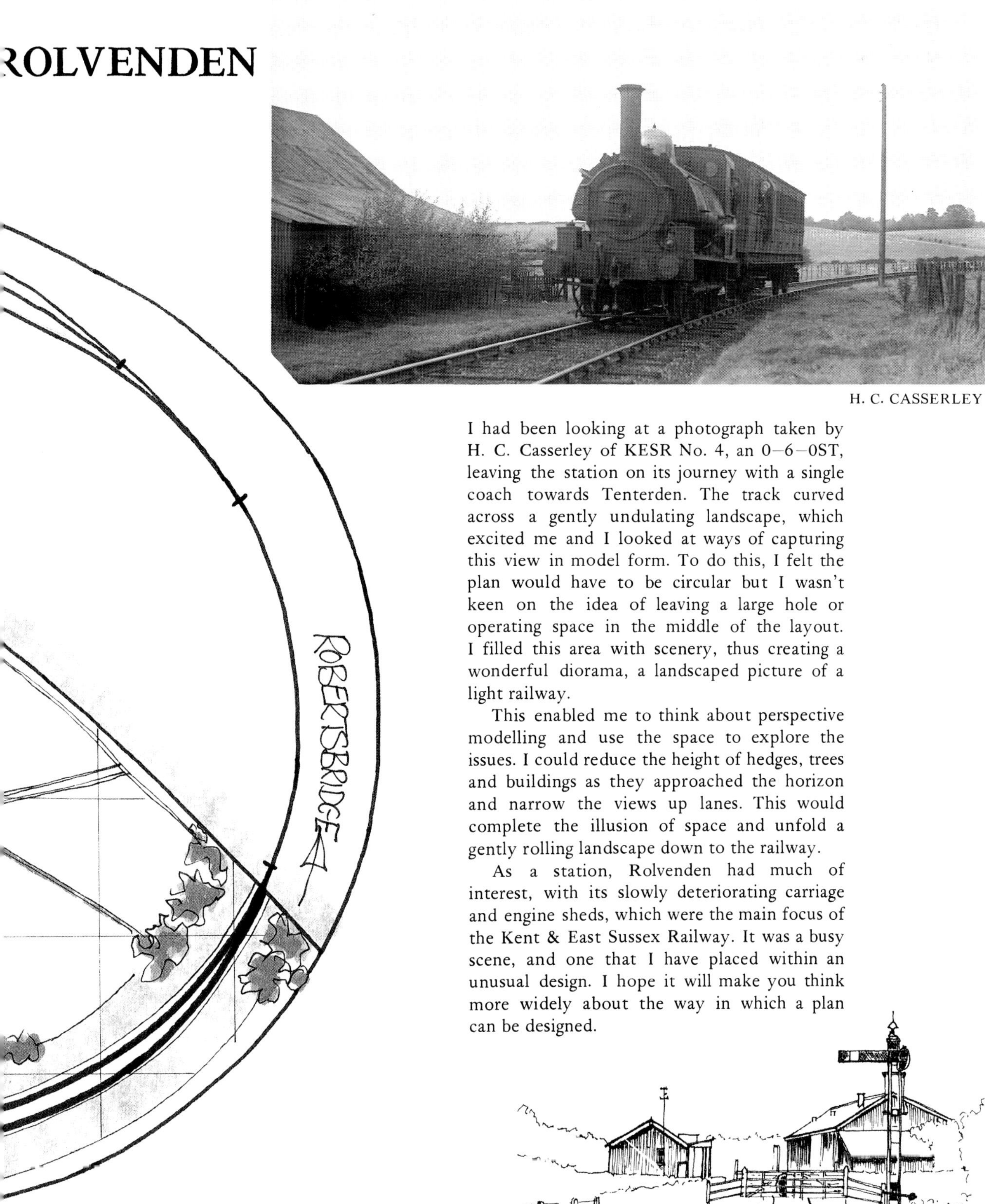

H. C. CASSERLEY

I had been looking at a photograph taken by H. C. Casserley of KESR No. 4, an 0–6–0ST, leaving the station on its journey with a single coach towards Tenterden. The track curved across a gently undulating landscape, which excited me and I looked at ways of capturing this view in model form. To do this, I felt the plan would have to be circular but I wasn't keen on the idea of leaving a large hole or operating space in the middle of the layout. I filled this area with scenery, thus creating a wonderful diorama, a landscaped picture of a light railway.

This enabled me to think about perspective modelling and use the space to explore the issues. I could reduce the height of hedges, trees and buildings as they approached the horizon and narrow the views up lanes. This would complete the illusion of space and unfold a gently rolling landscape down to the railway.

As a station, Rolvenden had much of interest, with its slowly deteriorating carriage and engine sheds, which were the main focus of the Kent & East Sussex Railway. It was a busy scene, and one that I have placed within an unusual design. I hope it will make you think more widely about the way in which a plan can be designed.

I liked the stone and thatch cottages that graced the hillside behind the station at Chisledon, but, as I wanted to develop a 7mm scale model, it seemed inevitable that some major pruning of the track layout would be necessary. Like Lydham, much of the interest lies at one end of the station, and this for me was the area I wished to focus upon. It appeared sensible to leave out the pointwork (This could be replaced by a pivoting fiddle yard), thereby reducing the length of the model considerably. Scenically, this part of the station

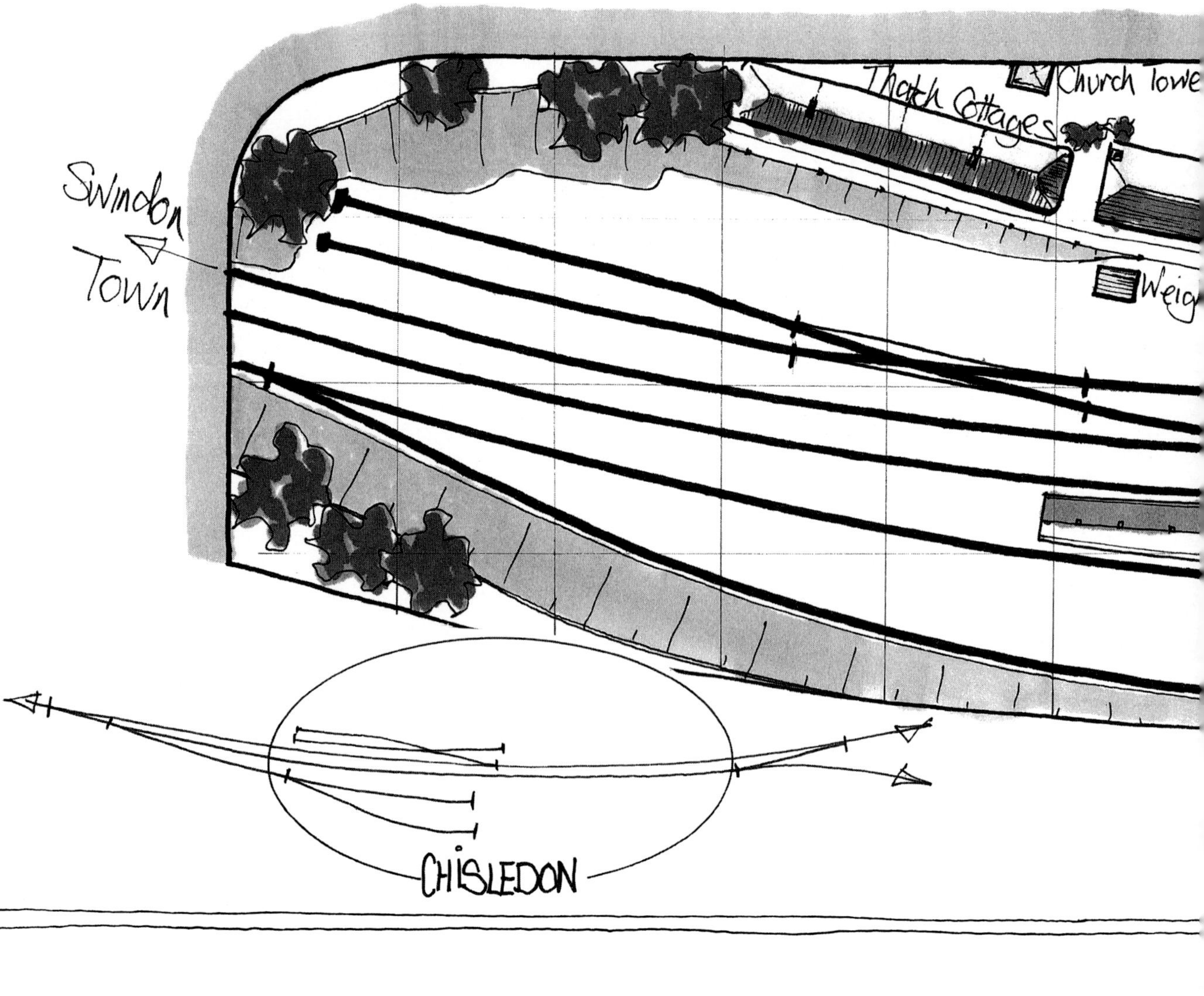

CHISLEDON

ıs attractive, but my attention was always awn more to the charming limestone cottages ıich overlooked the platforms and goods yard.

This inevitable slicing-up of the prototype an leaves a rather strange track layout, but ıat is left is logical and can be operated proto- pically. Attention is directed clearly at the ost interesting features – station building and atforms, signal box, goods yards, cottages and e Elm Tree Inn. Each of these could be veloped into a cameo or small scene, where tailing would grab the eye: a curtain blowing om an open window, or a flicker of firelight ncing across a neatly modelled front room ould attract you towards the cottages. At the m Tree Inn, a shaft of sunlight may catch a mpse of wire wheels and chrome headlamps thin the darkness of the barn, stimulating terest and intrigue.

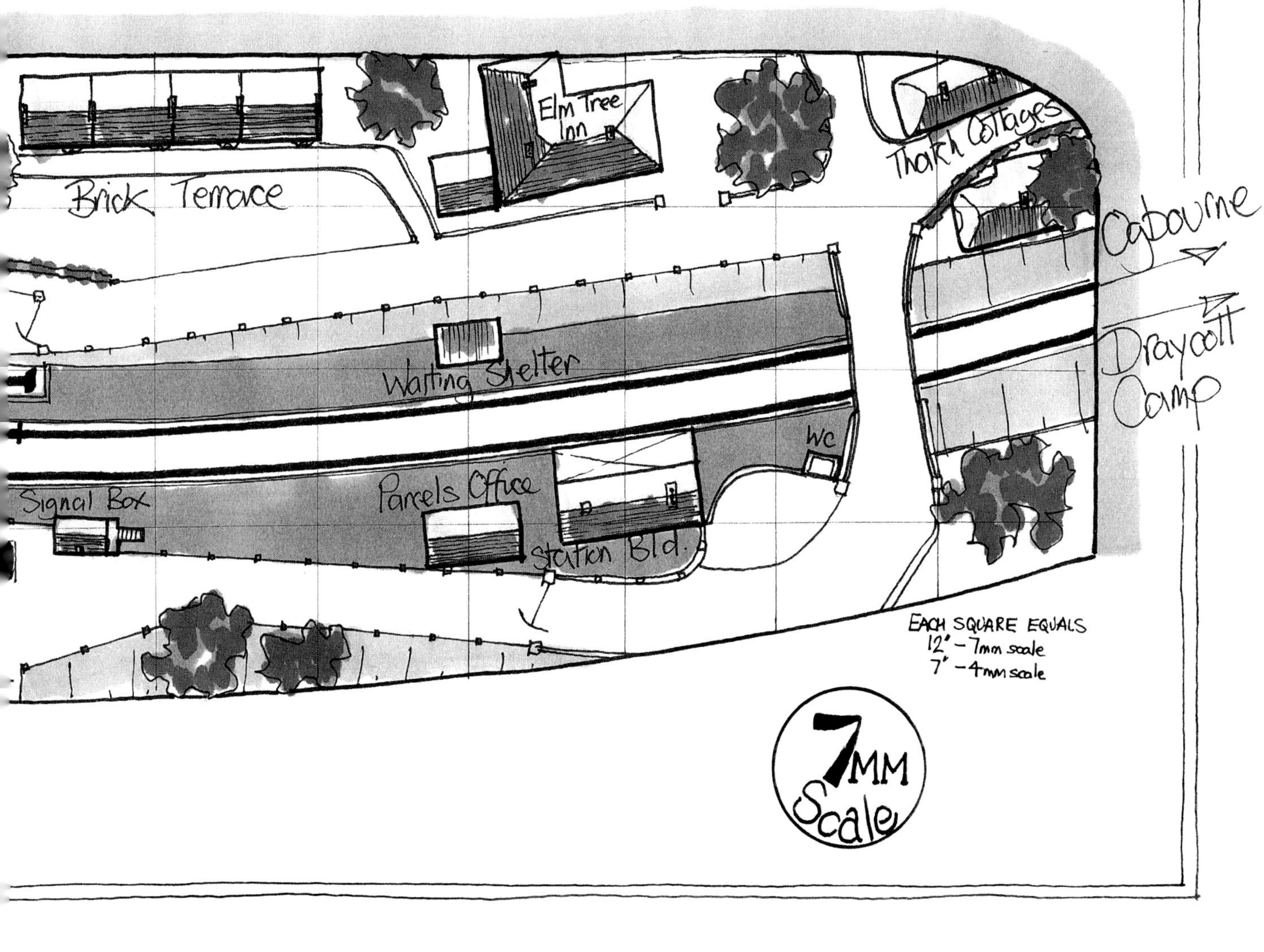

A view of Keith Armes's 2mm scale model of Bliss Mill, behind which departing trains slip from our gaze at Chipping Norton, brings this book to a close. It also reminds me to say a very big thank you to all those layout builders, like Keith Armes, whose inspiring models I have shown between these pages. My thoughts have been influenced by all of them, as well as other mentors like Peter Denny, David Jenkinson and Frank Dyer and those more recent, like Martyn Welch and Gordon Gravett.

A very special thank you also goes to Paul Karau for his untiring enthusiasm, trust and friendship. He has sensitively pieced together my text, photographs, plans and drawings into a book that I am very proud of. Finally, without the support of Gill I wouldn't have been able to write this volume, much of which was mulled over as I strolled across muddy Northamptonshire fields with my constant companion, Rags. To all these people I say thank you.

Barry Norman
Southwick